A MAN OF MANY FLAGS

M Cherif Bassiouni was a towering figure in international law. He was personally connected to some of the most historically relevant moments of the past century: the Suez War; the Camp David Accords; the fall of Muammar el-Qaddafi in Libya and the establishment of the International Criminal Court. A true global citizen – raised in Egypt, educated in Europe and emigrated to the United States – his life cut across cultures and religions. This fascinating memoir gives an immediate and personal eye-witness account of the operation of international events during a tumultuous period.

A Man of Many Flags

Memoirs of a War Crimes Investigator

M Cherif Bassiouni

·HART·

OXFORD · LONDON · NEW YORK · NEW DELHI · SYDNEY

HART PUBLISHING

Bloomsbury Publishing Plc

Kemp House, Chawley Park, Cumnor Hill, Oxford, OX2 9PH, UK

1385 Broadway, New York, NY 10018, USA

HART PUBLISHING, the Hart/Stag logo, BLOOMSBURY and the Diana logo are
trademarks of Bloomsbury Publishing Plc

First published in Great Britain 2020

A catalogue record for this book is available from the British Library.

Library of Congress Cataloging-in-Publication data

Names: Bassiouni, M. Cherif, 1937–2017, author.

Title: A man of many flags : memoirs of a war crimes investigator/M Cherif Bassiouni.

Description: Chicago : Hart Publishing, an imprint of Bloomsbury Publishing, 2020. |
Includes bibliographical references and index.

Identifiers: LCCN 2019048485 | ISBN 9781509934492 (hardcover) |
ISBN 9781509934508 (Epub)

Subjects: LCSH: Criminal investigation (International law) | War crimes investigation. |
Wars—Personal narratives.

Classification: LCC KZ7390 .B37 2020 | DDC 363.25/938092 [B]—dc23

LC record available at https://lccn.loc.gov/2019048485

ISBN: HB: 978-1-50993-449-2
        ePDF: 978-1-50993-451-5
        ePub: 978-1-50993-450-8

Typeset by Compuscript Ltd, Shannon

To find out more about our authors and books visit www.hartpublishing.co.uk. Here you will find extracts,
author information, details of forthcoming events and the option to sign up for our newsletters.

About the Author

M. Cherif Bassiouni was a lifelong advocate of international criminal justice and human rights law. He dedicated his life to promoting these human values and to sharing his passion with others.

Bassiouni began his law career at DePaul University College of Law in Chicago, Illinois, where he taught for forty-five years. A founder of both the International Human Rights Law Institute at DePaul and the Siracusa Institute for Criminal Justice and Human Rights in Siracusa, Italy, Bassiouni shared his dedication for international criminal justice and human rights with students, academics, judges, and lawyers throughout the world.

He held numerous positions with the United Nations, the United States and other governments, and non-governmental organizations. He was the recipient of awards and honors from many governments and academic institutions, including a nomination for the 1999 Nobel Peace Prize for his work on the establishment of the International Criminal Court.

A prolific author, Bassiouni wrote and edited seventy-seven academic books and more than 250 articles throughout his career. *A Man of Many Flags: Memoirs of a War Crimes Investigator & Human Rights Champion* is his first and only memoir.

To my Lisetta & Ellie

Foreword

I
T IS AN honor for me to have been invited to 'pen a little something' for the memoir of my dear departed friend, Professor Cherif Bassiouni. He was certainly one of the most prodigious and productive writers in the field of international criminal law. Since I am now in my hundredth year, I am grateful that I have not been requested to write a brief summary of Cherif's many outstanding works.

Cherif was a courageous and ardent champion of justice for all. His personal contribution to advancing the rule of law is immeasurable. He was mindful of the many shortcomings of existing practices and the continuing need to enforce the protection of human rights universally. His many books, articles, lectures and leadership roles in several important international legal societies served as indispensible catalysts in the evolutionary development of a more humane and rational world social order.

I am particularly grateful for his joining with me in seeking to overcome objections to penalizing the crime of aggression by condemning the illegal use of armed force as a 'crime against humanity.'

We are all indebted to Cherif for his selfless dedication and tireless striving for a more humane world, governed by the rule of internationally binding and enforceable laws. We still have a long way to go but Cherif's contribution helped move us closer to our shared goals. He did not live in vain.

Sincerely,
Ben Ferencz
Chief Prosecutor
The Einsatzgruppen Case
Nuremberg Military Tribunals

Acknowledgements

WE NEED TO remind ourselves that a memoir is not an autobiography. Hence this account is incomplete, with important events unmentioned. While Cherif wrote some "memoir thoughts" several years ago, the serious writing began only about seven months before he passed away on September 25, 2017. He wrote and then dictated most of this work during his last four months of life.

My thanks to all who encouraged him to 'Write your memoirs!' His dear friends Ekk Müller-Rappard and Reynald Ottenhof were often giving him gentle reminders. His staff at his Siracusa Institute were always encouraging, with special thanks to Gabriele Pulvirenti for his work in adding a section of Cherif's speeches to the Institute's website. All his "adoptees," Kelly McCracken Pembleton, Mohamed Helal, Khaled Ahmed, Laith Saud, Yaser Tabbara, and Ahmed Rehab, frequently asked, 'How's the writing going?' Two good friends, Dr. Richardo Davison and the late Dr. Barrie Richmond, were also strong encouragers. His stepsons, Andrew Klemen and Mark Klemen, thought his memoirs would be a really great read and told him so. He also had the constant love and support of his daughter, Lisa Capitanini. And so much gratitude goes to Rosa Ortega for keeping the home together no matter who was visiting, staying over or popping in unexpectedly. The medical care from Dr. Regina Stein and Dr. Patrick Gallagher was simply excellent.

Cherif and I had several conversations over his last months as he struggled to decide how much personal or intimate information to include. He ultimately chose to include very little, in part because he was a very private person and in part because he said he truly did not know how to write about intimate events or feelings, and he realized he had no time to learn a new form of writing.

My thanks go to all who have helped this project materialize. To Philip Morris International, without whose generous grant the memoirs would not have happened. Profound thanks to Deirdre McGrory and Daniel Swift, Cherif's assistants, two most capable attorneys who were with him every working day for five years until his death. They answered phones, took dictations, assisted with the memoirs, and all sorts of other duties, and they did so willingly and helpfully. After his death, they took on the huge task of fact-checking everything mentioned in his memoirs:

difficult painstaking work, done perfectly. My gratitude to Ben Ferencz, a decades long friend, who contributed the forward: Ben and Cherif had much in common and held each other in deep and warm regard. Louisa Williams is simply one of the best editors we could ever hope for – a true gem. And to the publisher, Hart Publishing, my gratitude.

M. Cherif Bassiouni was one of the most fascinating people one could ever hope to meet. His influence in international criminal and human rights law was and still is profound. Someday a complete (or more complete) biography will be available. Until then we have his memoirs.

Rest in peace, my love.

Elaine Klemen-Bassiouni

Contents

"The world rests on three pillars:
on truth, on justice and on peace."
Rabban Simeon ben Gamaliel.

*

"If you see a wrong, you must right it:
with your hand if you can, or, with your words,
or with your stare, or with your heart
and that is the weakest of faith."
Prophet Mohammad

*

"If you want peace, work for justice."
Pope Paul IV

April 1993: The Former Yugoslavia

From the Soviet-built Antonov plane, I could hear the shots almost before I could see the city of Sarajevo.

On the short flight from Zagreb, I sat on a small wooden bench with William Fenrick, my Canadian colleague on the United Nations Commission of Experts appointed to investigate violations of international humanitarian law in the former Yugoslavia, and listened to the grinding noise of metal scraping metal as three armoured personnel carriers shifted in the hull of the plane. While this was certainly not the first time that gunfire had been directed my way, I suspected that the Serb mortars and artillery were intended more to scare than harm us.

By the time we landed in Sarajevo it was late in the night of 24 April 1993, and we headed directly to our hotel, hoping to catch up on sleep so we could hit the ground running for our first day of field operations the following morning. The Holiday Inn in Sarajevo showed many scars of conflict: just through the glass doors of its faded yellow façade, we found rows of cots lining the lobby, which, we were told, was safer than the floors above. After I explained that I was not thrilled about sleeping among strangers, the proprietor offered me the choice of Room 727 or 725. Being partial to the number seven, I chose the first.

The hotel had good reason to put its guests in the lobby: all the windows in Room 727 were shattered, and plastic sheets hung over the broken panes. There was no electricity, water or working toilet. But there was a bed with a mattress, two pillows and two blankets, and that was all I really needed to get through the night. Despite an artillery barrage not too far from the hotel, I quickly settled in and dozed off.

I still do not know if it was the building shaking or the sound of mortar shells connecting with concrete that pulled me from sleep, but I knew instantly that the hotel had been hit. I rolled off my bed onto the cold floor and pulled the mattress on top of me to serve as thin protection. After about five minutes, which seemed to last a lifetime, the artillery barrage ended and I felt safe enough to leave my room to try to determine what had happened.

Outside Room 727 I encountered newly exposed concrete and electrical wires dangling from what had been Room 725. Lieutenant-Colonel Anton Kempenaars, my Dutch military aide for the field investigation, grabbed a flashlight and came to find me. We surveyed the damage and photographed the new holes in the wall.

The 1930s and 1940s: Cairo, Egypt

THE 1930S IN Egypt was still a time when almost all marriages were arranged between families and not necessarily the product of two people falling in love and choosing to have a life and family together. My parents were no exception. Their marriage was arranged by their families, both wealthy and prominent, both with attorneys at the helm.

Their wedding in October 1936 was the society event of the year and one of the most sensational weddings held in Egypt. Always a social woman with scores of friends around her, my mother had twelve bridesmaids, one of whom, Farida, a classmate and close friend, later became the first wife of the Egyptian King Farouk. A photograph of my parents on their wedding day always hung in my home office; even in the small black-and-white photograph, the sheer opulence of the event comes across, as the young couple poses surrounded by arrays of white flowers in all shapes and sizes. They quickly became a well-known and admired couple in Egyptian high society and led a life of prestige and social prominence.

I was born on 9 December 1937. A year later, after my father was appointed vice-consul to the New York consulate, my mother went with him to the United States while I stayed with my maternal grandmother. My parents lived lavishly in New York, renting a fabulous apartment on Park Avenue, with a car and a chauffeur. They lived the high life of 1930s society, and by most accounts were loved by everyone around them, who considered them exotic and beautiful. My mother, Amina, had very dark hair and very dark eyes. She was a stunning model of an Arab woman. She and my father, Ibrahim, who had wavy blondish hair and blue eyes, appeared quite the pair. They were both great dancers and loved socialising, so they enjoyed their time among the *beau monde* in New York, although it was to be short-lived.

In 1940, as US convoys to England began to come under attack from the Germans, my parents returned to Egypt. By 1942, there was great fear that the Germans would occupy Egypt, as the British were suffering major defeats.

I had spent the first years of my life being raised by my maternal grandmother and my nanny, both Austrian, so was lacking a father figure. However, even after my parents returned to Cairo, my father was heavily involved in working in the office of the Ministry of Foreign Affairs, and I seldom saw him. My mother tried to keep our life as normal as possible, despite the war that Adolf Hitler and the British were fighting 'right in our backyard', as she put it. She made the effort to keep up a social calendar, hosting parties at night and inviting people for afternoon tea.

When guests arrived, my mother would have me stand next to her at the door and greet people. 'Say hello to Uncle Malik. Say good evening to Aunt Hathor', she would tell me. Most of these people I'd never met before, but it was the custom to call adults 'Uncle' or 'Aunt', and I complied with a bow. After I greeted her guests, my mother would usher me off to my grandmother and nanny, and one or other of them would often read to me from the *Tales of Struwwelpeter* or the Brothers Grimm. When I taxed their patience, my grandmother or nanny would tell me to play with my toys while they kept one eye in my direction and busied themselves with this or that. Sometimes I would manage to slip away and find a nice quiet spot where I could sit unobserved and eavesdrop on my mother and her guests. Our visitors spoke in languages I understood and those I did not. How many languages existed in the world, I wondered. How many could there be?

At my mother's parties, the words seemed to dance around the room like moths with musical wings and flit past my hiding place. Often the gathering would start with cheerful talk and laughter. I loved to listen to these bright words like bits of sunshine flashing here and there. But during these years, the early 1940s, the talk eventually turned dark, filled with silences between the words, blocks of space that seemed to ache as the talk turned to war. I tried to understand this word in all the languages I heard: war, krieg, harb, guerre. All the conversation turned around the war, whether it be in Europe or in North Africa, and there was nothing frivolous about it. I struggled to take its measure: people were fighting each other, but why? Was it like in the cowboy movies my father would sometimes take me to see, where one man tried to steal another's horse or cheat at cards? And here in Egypt, why were they fighting on our land, our soil? I posed this question to my father one day. He told me that both sides wanted our Suez Canal that connected the Red Sea and the Mediterranean Sea. The side that won the Suez Canal would win the war, he told me.

I had once visited the Suez Canal with my father, who explained to me that this was a marvel of engineering, that man had made this passage to join two seas. Without this canal, people would have to journey around the entire African continent and the Cape of Good Hope, which at the time would be a minimum of fifteen days of sailing, to reach Europe. I tried to act impressed by what my father told me, but to me it was just a body of water that did not look so different from the water in the River Nile that we passed each day. What was the difference between the river that men had made and the river that God had made? Ships passed through each, but people inexplicably wanted to fight over the river that men had made.

Sometimes at my mother's afternoon teas I heard people whispering as if their words were too horrible to be uttered, even across the teacups. In the lowest of low voices, they spoke of innocent people killed by the thousand. From my concealed vantage point, I heard the words, no matter how quietly spoken. At these times, I wished that both my grandfathers were alive because I was sure that they could save all those poor, innocent people, as they did in my bedtime stories. At the time, I did not understand that all of Europe was involved in the war started by Hitler in an effort to dominate and control the continent and beyond, while he and the Nazis slaughtered millions of Jews, along with Slavs, Roma, and others, in events we would later call the Holocaust.

More whispers. How was it that we were in the middle of a war that was not of our making? The British were all around us. They had been fighting Hitler's army for three years but had not managed to win. These were the rhetorical questions those adults around me posed, and I would darkly wonder whether Hitler wanted our canal so he could drop all the innocent people in the world into it and drown them, drown and kill all the good people in the world so there were no good people left. Someone had to stop Hitler once and for all, I decided. The British with their English words and English ways had not done the job.

September 1942: Cairo

I SOON HAD my chance: day was fading into night and I, a typical 4-year-old, was doing everything I could to elude my nanny's grasp and avoid going to bed. Just then the air raid sirens began. I had grown accustomed to the sirens' piercing noise and continued my childish antics until suddenly everything went black and I felt as if someone had wrapped me in a dark, unwanted blanket. I looked out the window and saw a full moon hanging in the sky, like the one the cow jumped over in the poem my English tutor would make me recite.

'Where's the child? Where's the child?' my mother screamed. She raced into my room and groped in the blackness until she found me. Then she scooped me in her arms and rushed toward the front door of our apartment, my grandmother and nanny scrambling along behind us.

My mother flung open the door and we hit a wall of darkness. We couldn't see, but we could hear people screaming and shouting and shuffling down the stairs. We joined the mass of frightened tenants streaming toward the basement for safety – pushed, jostled and squeezed from all sides. Nevertheless, I could hear the approaching aircraft throbbing above the noise. Just then, we were pushed from behind and my mother stumbled, and suddenly I was on the ground. I saw the doorway rimmed in moonlight and I ran toward it, threading through men's legs and around women's skirts as I tried to reach the outside.

It did not take long before I was through the door and standing in the street. Moonlight lit up the aircraft flying overhead. I looked straight up at the black marks under the wings that looked like the letter 'X' from my alphabet book. I ran into the street, pulled my toy gun from my holster, and began to shoot at the planes, taking aim and blasting away with all my might.

I heard my mother scream, 'My child! My child!' Then I was lifted in the air. My mother held me to her and rushed toward the building.

'Cherif, what were you doing?' she asked. 'Why did you run away?'

'I had to', I told her.

'But why?'

'I had to kill Uncle Hitler.'

I felt my mother's sobs as she held me tight and raced back through the door of our building and clambered down the steps to the basement. We edged through the darkness until my mother found a place for us on the floor. We could hear the aircraft, and we could hear the screaming bombs one after another. Again, I fired my pistol in the darkness at Uncle Hitler – starting down the path that led me in my grandfathers' footsteps: a lifetime of taking aim at bad men doing bad things to good people.

That night was one of the earliest and certainly clearest memories of my childhood, and I can still picture the aircraft above me and the sound of my mother yelling frantically. What I did not know at the time was that the night I tried to shoot down Uncle Hitler was the night of the second battle of El Alamein, the turning point of World War Two in northern Africa. The colonisation of northern Africa by European powers meant that when World War Two broke out, the region was already home to military forces, although the British Allied forces in the area protecting Egypt were far outnumbered by the scores of Italian and Italian colonial troops. In September 1940, Italian forces began to make their way toward Egypt from Libya, with the goal of invading and occupying Egypt to gain control of the Suez Canal. The Italians were initially unsuccessful in their endeavours to take control of Tobruk, a Libyan port city on the Mediterranean close to the border with Egypt. In early February 1941, German Field Marshal Erwin Rommel arrived in Libya to command German forces sent to reinforce the Italians. Rommel successfully led the Axis forces to the Egyptian border by mid-April 1941, resulting in a stalemate between the opposing armies, followed by a successful British attack on Rommel's position and the pushback of Axis forces.

Then, in early 1942, Rommel launched a second offensive, reaching just west of Tobruk in only two weeks. Another Axis offensive followed in May 1942, taking Tobruk and pursuing Allied forces into Egypt; by July 1942 this advance had got all the way to El Alamein. With only 115 kilometers lying between El Alamein and Alexandria, the Axis powers were close to taking the Suez Canal and all that would come with it. But at El Alamein the British were able to halt the advance.

The strategic importance of the Suez Canal and control of Egypt could not be overstated. The Suez Canal connected Britain with its overseas territories, providing access for oil from the Middle East and raw materials from Asia – all of which was necessary to sustain military forces and win the war. Allied control of Egypt and the Suez Canal was also vital to the lives of Jews living in Palestine and attempting to reach there from all over Europe in hopes of finding safety from the Holocaust.[1] Everything in life is relative, as I can see now, and for Europeans at the time the European theatre of war was the most important because it was a matter of life and death. What was happening in the African campaign seemed relatively minor in comparison, notwithstanding its strategic location, but for many Jews it was a matter of survival. From Alexandria to Port Said is only about 250 kilometers; after crossing the Suez Canal, the Axis forces would be able to enter Palestine freely. About 300,000 Jews lived there at the time, with a constant influx of Jewish refugees from Europe. If the Germans occupied Palestine, it would lead not only to the extermination of the Jews there but also to the destruction of an escape route for the Jews of Europe. This was an enormous worry for those concerned about Jews, let alone those who believed in eventually establishing a Jewish state.

Hence the lives of the Jews living in Palestine and those seeking to flee Europe depended almost entirely on the success of the Allied troops fighting Rommel's forces in North Africa, and it all came down to the second battle of El Alamein, the confrontation that pitted Field Marshal Rommel and Lieutenant-General Bernard Montgomery. Although events did not go exactly according to plan, Montgomery outnumbered Rommel in troops and weaponry and was finally able to push the Axis forces back and force a retreat. I did not know it at the time I took aim at Uncle Hitler, but that night was life-changing, not only for myself but for the war in North Africa, for the Jews seeking refuge in Palestine, and in some ways for all of humanity.

---

[1] As many as 51,000 Jews were legally allowed to immigrate to Mandate Palestine by the British between 1939 and 1944. It is estimated that over another 100,000 Jews attempted to immigrate illegally between 1934 and 1948. Over 50,000 were intercepted by the British Navy and sent to various detention camps. In addition, between 1931 and 1947 the Jewish population of Palestine rose from 175,000 to 630,000. American-Israeli Cooperative Enterprise, 'Immigration to Israel: British Restrictions on Jewish Immigration to Palestine (1919–1942)' *Jewish Virtual Library*, https://www.jewishvirtuallibrary.org/british-restrictions-on-jewish-immigration-to-palestine.

September and November 1991: Siracusa, Italy

I FIRST HEARD personal accounts of the horrors taking place in the former Yugoslavia months before the war fully broke out across the region. I was in Italy, directing a seminar on international law at the Siracusa Institute, when I met a participant from what was then Yugoslavia. The young man, a Croat, was a professor at the University of Zagreb. The professor came to me one day and asked, 'Are you aware of what is happening in Vukovar? Do you know that Vukovar is surrounded?'

My honest reply was surely not what he had hoped for: I told him I didn't even know where Vukovar was.

He quickly explained that Vukovar, in Croatia, was surrounded by Serbs.

Why were Serbs in Croatia, I asked.

'The war', he said. 'You know ...' He took a deep breath. 'We're at war in Croatia.'

The young man told me that Vukovar, where many of his relatives lived, still had about 1,000 fighting men but was surrounded by about 10,000 men, including some known to exterminate people. I had no idea this was going on.

In the next few days, I learned much more about the situation in Croatia, in part through many telephone calls with the young man's family and friends in the besieged city that he graciously let me listen in on. Those on the other end of the telephone line described the siege, the battle, the terror and the violence going on around them. As I listened and heard the gunshots in the background, my mind returned to my own experience in the 1956 Suez War.

I will never forget the last phone call I listened to between the young professor and his relatives in Vukovar. We heard cannon shots in the background, and then the phone line went dead. We knew then that the city had fallen.

* * *

The Balkans had been plagued by conflict and tensions long before I arrived there in the early 1990s. The ethnic tensions that had been brewing for centuries quickly began tearing apart communities, from major cities to rural hamlets. Former friends, classmates and neighbours committed heinous acts against each other based solely on ethnic identity. Civilians throughout the region, along with those actively engaged in combat, were brutalised. In fact, many of the horrors relatively unique to the conflict, including rape as an act of ethnic cleansing, the use of mass graves and the shelling of civilian cities, were documented only after my fellow commission members and I arrived in the region and began our work.

While the region's ethnic tensions were centuries old, the newly erupting violence began to attract international attention in 1991, and by 1992, the United Nations had begun to employ sanctions in hopes of quashing the violence, a tactic that it continued to use throughout the conflict. By the autumn of 1992, enough pressure had been mounted on the UN Security Council to investigate the allegations of war crimes and crimes against humanity in the Balkan region that Resolution 780 was adopted, establishing an investigative commission to document the commission of war crimes and other violations of international humanitarian law. On 6 October 1992, the resolution was adopted. So began my decades-long connection with the former Yugoslavia.

October 1992: Chicago, United States

MONTHS AFTER I returned from my time in Siracusa, on the morning of 10 October 1992, I was working in my office at DePaul University in Chicago when I received a phone call from Ambassador Nabil El-Arabi, a longtime friend who was then the permanent representative of Egypt to the United Nations. El-Arabi excitedly told me that the United Nations had established a commission to investigate war crimes in the former Yugoslavia as a prelude to an international criminal court. He had just seen the UN Secretary-General, Boutros Boutros-Ghali, a mutual friend, who had told El-Arabi 'I'm going to appoint Cherif to it. This is something he has been working on for the last twenty years.' Was my dream of the creation of an international criminal court finally coming true?

As I sat back in my chair trying to process what I had just heard, I realised that I had not asked El-Arabi for basic information such as the nature of the commission and the scope of its mandate. Boutros-Ghali had not been exaggerating when he had said I had working on the idea of an international criminal court for more than two decades, so these were important questions, not just for my potential role in the commission but for my general thinking about what might be next for international criminal justice. So, in hopes of finding some answers, I reached out to colleagues and friends at the United Nations, and I soon had a faxed copy of UN Security Council Resolution 780.

The text was clear. The United Nations had indeed established an independent investigatory agency with the broadest mandate since the trials at Nuremburg. I was elated at the idea and hoped that this might be the breakthrough that could pave the way for a permanent international criminal court.

After working myself into a bit of a frenzy, I collected myself for a few minutes of meditation and prayer, thanking God for allowing me to be part of something so significant and asking for guidance to do what was right for justice and for the victims of the conflict. Throughout all my work on the commission, I tried to keep these goals, focusing on justice and helping those harmed by war, uppermost in my mind. Unfortunately, that accounted for many of my later difficulties with some governments and senior UN bureaucrats.

October 1942: Cairo

I N EGYPT IN the early 1940s, life went on tensely. Father was always busy with work and worry. Mother was forever trying to keep up our spirits with festivities. As a child, I knew nothing of dates and time; time was just a block of now-ness. But even so, I could sense the constant anxiety.

In mid-October 1942, my father came home for lunch in the afternoon and informed my mother that he and she would not be going out that evening. My mother had been looking forward to attending this particular reception and was disappointed about missing it, but my father was firm: he had to meet somebody for a confidential diplomatic discussion.

Later that afternoon, the doorbell rang, and my father told my mother that he and his guest should not be interrupted and that neither she nor the child (meaning me), should make any noise while he and his visitor were talking.

My mother, being the woman that she was, decided to sneak a peek from behind the curtains to see who this mysterious guest was, and I huddled next to her, filled with a young boy's curiosity. We saw someone who, in my recollection, must have been no more than around 5 foot 6, short for a man, and stocky in build. As far as appearances go, the man seemed innocuous, the sort who could stand in the middle of an empty room and never be noticed.

My father took the visitor into a small room attached to our larger living room but left the door ajar. At one point, while the man and my father were drinking tea, the man took off his jacket, rolled up his sleeve, showed my father a tattooed number, and described a place he repeatedly referred to as Auschwitz. My mother and I, still hidden, were both curious about the man's tattoo, but my mother soon realized what it was and began sobbing.

As my father escorted the man out, my father also had tears in his eyes. I remember that after the guest left, my parents sat in the stillness of the living room. I sat with them, not understanding what had transpired. Eventually my mother turned to me and said, 'You know about the bad man in Europe named Hitler. Well, he takes certain people, and he kills them.'

'Why would he do that?' I asked.

'It's difficult to understand, but he doesn't like certain types of people', she said. My mother told me of the friends she had who were

Jewish and reminded me about their children, who were my friends. She then explained how Hitler would take people like these friends, put them in prisons, tattoo them and eventually kill them. I heard the name Hitler repeated several times but did not understand much except that this bad man, Hitler, was killing Jews and others as a butcher kills animals. This impressed me deeply because I was terrified of butchers, having once seen the head of a rabbit cut off in a butcher's shop. The tattoo on the man's arm reminded me, too, of the red numbers painted onto the fur of camels herded to their slaughter through the streets of Cairo. This butcher called Hitler was doing such a thing to people? To women like my mother and grandmother? To children like my cousin and kindergarten classmates and me? Impossible – but the tattoo?

I later learned that my father's visitor was involved in the formation of an all-Jewish brigade fighting the Germans.[2] I remember thinking how anachronistic it was that here were the Brits, fighting the Germans to – at least in part – protect the Jews, and yet they segregated the Jewish brigade from the rest of their servicemen. In any case, the man had been captured and held at Auschwitz but had managed to escape. He then volunteered to go twice inside German lines to gather information for the British. That year, 1942, the Jewish Agency for Palestine sent him to Egypt to lobby on behalf of the creation of an independent Jewish state. I am unsure what, if any, help my father was able to provide this man with his task to find safe harbour for Jews escaping Europe, but that day remained with me forever.[3]

---

[2] *Editor's note:* It seems unlikely that the collection of characteristics and personal experiences that Professor Bassiouni attributes to this one man could all refer to one person, and it is worth noting that the account of this man's visit comes from the recollection of a 4-year-old child. Nonetheless, given the extraordinary circumstances of his childhood, it is likely that Professor Bassiouni heard all these stories in his home, among his father's diplomatic circle, during the Second World War.

[3] By this time, Jewish migration from Europe into Palestine had already begun, although it was not yet in full flux. The Europeans euphemistically referred to the phenomenon as 'displacement'. I have often found that with human tragedies resulting from political issues, people tag those tragedies in euphemistic, non-descriptive terms. For example, when Korean women were captured during war and taken as sex slaves, they were – for years – referred to as 'comfort women', a deeply inappropriate term for sexual slavery, which is, without question, one of the worst things to which a human being can be subjected. And so the Jews of Europe became 'displaced persons', and later on, the crisis was referred to, again euphemistically, as 'the Jewish Question', rather than what it was: genocide and ethnic cleansing. This has bothered me over the years because it adds to the dehumanisation of what victims suffer. The concern of the advocates of the Jewish Agency, and of those in Palestine trying to find an accommodation with the Palestinians and with the British occupying forces, was that if the British lost, they would be subjected to the Germans – and once again face extermination.

April 1993: The Former Yugoslavia

THE UN COMMISSION of Experts began its fieldwork in April 1993. Commission members Bill Fenrick of Canada, Frits Kalshoven of the Netherlands, and I spent some time investigating the possible commission of war crimes in Zagreb and Belgrade before making our way to Sarajevo, although Kalshoven chose not to accompany us to any areas of conflict and stayed behind in the relative peace of Slovenia. After we landed in Sarajevo and had a less-than-restful night's stay at the Holiday Inn, Fenrick and I regrouped the next morning, ready to take on our enormous task.

The bombardment of a civilian city is a war crime, and so during our investigation in Sarajevo that first morning, 25 April, I set out to establish a system to keep count of how many shells fell on the city and how many people were killed and injured each day. Later in the morning, Fenrick and I visited the State Hospital and toured a makeshift operation room housed in the basement of the building, where doctors hoped it might be shielded from the mortar and artillery shelling raining down on the city. We heard of the immense difficulty of treating the sick and wounded in a facility that was lacking staff, equipment and medicine (including painkillers) while under constant fear of attack. Surgeries were performed by gaslight, with no anaesthetic available. The sounds coming from the pained and the injured were beyond anything I had ever experienced.

That afternoon, at a clinic where rape victims received care, we met a psychiatrist who introduced us to two young women, one 16 years old and the other 17. I noticed that they were nicely dressed and wearing a touch of makeup. This might seem unremarkable anywhere else, but to me, these young women were human nature at its best, individuals maintaining their dignity during the most difficult times imaginable. In a city without running water, anyone wearing a clean shirt had probably had risked their life to find a way to wash it. No stores were open to sell cosmetics, so a homemade substitute must have sufficed for a hint of lipstick.

The young women's perseverance and tenacity became even more impressive as they shared their story. They explained where they came from and told us about their families. They were, they said, two of eight girls who had been captured by Serb militias and held hostage outside Foča, in Bosnia-Herzegovina. Their families had fled, and the girls, aged between 11 and 16 at the time, were held for eight months until their parents were able to pay a ransom to their Serbian captors. During those eight months they were repeatedly raped and sexually assaulted by the militiamen and the captors' friends. They were also made to work as maids in their captors' homes and constantly threatened with being killed or being sent to a nearby Serb holding camp where many other women were raped.

The two women at the clinic told us that the first commander overseeing their confinement took part in their sexual abuse, but after he was killed, his replacement did not participate. On their last day in confinement, the day their ransom was to be paid, the women said, about twenty militiamen tried to get into the house to rape them and the other girls before they left, but the second commander stood in the doorway of the home and blocked the militiamen from entering.

Perhaps similar situations occurred elsewhere during the conflict in the former Yugoslavia, but this was the only case reported to the commission in which a Serb commander took affirmative action to prevent such horrific violations. Hearing this story, and others like it, was a constant reminder of how little the commission could actually help those in need – and how creating a lasting reminder of these people and their stories was all we could truly hope to provide.

When the young women finished speaking, I asked if they would be willing to testify in court about the events they had described. Their courage and determination were deeply impressive: despite all they had endured and all the warnings about how difficult testifying might be, they readily agreed. I promised them that their stories would not be forgotten.

March 1994: The Former Yugoslavia

UNFORTUNATELY, THE STORIES of the two young women were not unusual, and during our investigation focusing on allegations of rape and sexual violence, we heard other accounts that brought even the most seasoned among us to the breaking point.

One evening, a prosecutor from Canada who was working on the rape investigation came to me after a full day of conducting interviews. This woman, who had spent nine years prosecuting violent crimes in Canada, was in tears. She said she could not do the work anymore.

That day, she had interviewed a man on crutches, a Croat from Sarajevo who had been an enthusiastic soccer player. Soccer is huge in Sarajevo, he said, and almost everyone knew that the Croats generally beat the Serbs. He had married a Serbian woman with two daughters after her Bosnian husband had died, and they lived in the woman's apartment on the Serb side of Sarajevo, where the two opened a soccer-themed café. The man said he always thought of his wife's two daughters as his own children.

When the conflict broke out and the barriers went up, the man explained, he had not been worried because his wife was Serb, but one day a group of young Serb militiamen, aged 19–22, arrived at the apartment and took the man away. The militiamen broke both of the man's legs, telling him that now he could never play soccer again, never again beat the Serbs. The man was tortured for days, his beatings overseen by a former neighbour and close family friend. During the first day of his torture, the man said, his wife and stepdaughters, who were 8 and 13, were brought to the same location, where the man was forced to watch as his wife and stepdaughters were raped and tortured. After days of these atrocities, the younger stepdaughter's throat was slit. Over the course of the following week, his older stepdaughter and wife were killed the same way – all while the man, chained, was forced to watch.

The next day, I went looking for the man the Canadian had interviewed and learned that he had committed suicide, leaving behind a note saying that he had lived for the day when he could tell his story. Humbled by his bravery and moved by his determination not to let the horrific events suffered by his family go untold, I did my best to tell his story in my account of our investigation.

Later, when I delivered the Commission of Experts' Final Report to the Security Council, I went to see the Secretary-General to share the man's story with him, just as I had shared it with Richard Goldstone, the chief prosecutor of the International Criminal Tribunal for the Prosecution of Persons Responsible for Serious Violations of International Humanitarian Law Committed in the Territory of the Former Yugoslavia since 1991, or the ICTY, and Antonio Cassese, the ICTY's first president.

I told all three this man's story, noting that in his suicide note he had said he wanted his story to be known – and that I particularly wanted these three to know it. Cassese promised me that when he wrote the ICTY's first report to the Security Council, he would include the man's story. But the story did not make it into the report, probably to avoid accusations that the account was too graphic, as such stories often must be watered down to appease politicians and diplomats. But when such stories are forgotten or sanitised, people lose sight of the human sufferings of war and the harrowing effects of depersonalisation and dehumanisation.

1900s: Various Locations in Egypt

I WAS BORN into a wealthy, prominent Muslim Egyptian family, and I give its chronicle here because these familial roots and lore have always served to ballast or to check me, no matter where I have found myself. My paternal great-grandfather, Ibrahim Bassiouni, began his career as a water engineer. He was responsible for the irrigation system of southern Egypt, from Cairo all the way to the southern border with the Sudan. He worked in the early 1800s on the first Aswan dam between Egypt and the Sudan. Although he came from the small town called Bassioun in the Delta, he moved to the southern city of Asyut because that was where his work was located. His son, my paternal grandfather, Mahmoud Ibrahim Bassiouni, was an attorney. He led the Upper Egypt contingent of the 1919 Revolution against the British in an effort to get Egyptian independence and be free of colonial status as a British protectorate state. He was arrested by the British for his leadership role and was tried by a British military court, sentenced to death and confined to a western desert oasis. He appealed his conviction, which was ultimately reversed by the Privy Council. After his release and the British protectorate status over Egypt ended, he was elected to Egypt's first independent Senate in 1923. He served in the Senate, including some time as its president, until his death in 1946.

My father, Ibrahim Bassiouni, was born most probably in 1907 in Asyut and named after my paternal great-grandfather, his grandfather. My paternal grandmother, Wahiba Nagib, also came from Asyut, but both her mother and father were half-Turkish, and she was born with red hair and green eyes. Throughout her upbringing she was heavily steeped in Turkish traditions and educated according to Western conventions. Wahiba knew Turkish, French and Italian, and she played the piano from childhood. She loved the opera and memorised all the famous arias one could play on the piano. In the early days of my father's family, she taught each of her five children to play a musical instrument, and after dinner they would play together. It is perhaps because of his Turkish roots that my father, Ibrahim, was born with slightly blond hair and blue eyes.

Ibrahim was very much the darling of his mother, who spoiled him no end, perhaps to counter the rigid management of a long-time family caretaker known as Ibrahim the Sudanese. I remember Ibrahim the Sudanese as a tall, dark, strapping man who bore three scars on each side of his face, the result of razor cuts made by his parents in accordance with Sudanese tradition. Ibrahim, my grandfather, told his son that Ibrahim the Sudanese had his full authority, including household expenditures. Despite his mother's attempts to spoil him, my father was a very responsible child, most likely to the credit of Ibrahim the Sudanese's sternness, and he subsequently took care of his two younger brothers, Mahmoud and Ali, who were more difficult children.

My father went to school in Asyut and to the University of Cairo's School of Business. In 1924, he went to England, where he completed his master's studies in economics with honours from Leeds University in 1927, one of only seven people in England to graduate with such a degree that year. Grandmother Wahiba, being wealthy in her own right, gave him significant sums of money when he was there, enough that in 1925 he owned a Bugatti, which was one of the most fashionable and expensive sports cars of the time. By most accounts, he was well liked and probably enjoyed himself very much. He must have been quite a dandy; he enjoyed dancing, was great at the waltz, and knew all the modern dances of the day, the jitterbug and the quickstep, and whatever was popular in the 1920s. Yet he apparently was also disciplined in his studies.

Years later, when I worked up the courage to ask him whether he had a girlfriend in England, he told me about a young lady whom he had been very fond of and who had been very fond of him. When I asked why he hadn't married her, he gave me a simple answer: 'She didn't darn socks.'

My father explained that in our family, wives darn socks for their husbands, and she did not want to darn his socks. I was flabbergasted at the response but later realised that my father, being a master diplomat, did not want to speak ill of this woman, and so to avoid having to answer my question honestly, he came up with that absurd, simple answer.

When my father returned to Egypt, my grandfather was the president of the Senate, and with a prestigious and rare degree in economics, my father found a post in the Ministry of Finance as a senior inspector for fiscal tax matters, where he worked on the reform of the Egyptian tax codes. Sometime in 1936 or 1937, he was transferred to the Ministry of Foreign Affairs and because of his intellect and his father's connections immediately became part of the minister's staff.

My mother, too, came from a prominent family. Her great-grandfather, my great-great-grandfather, was raised in Turkey as a military officer and attended the prestigious Saint Cyr Academy in France. He was then sent to Egypt to tutor the sons of the khedive, the position of the then-ruler of Egypt appointed by the Ottoman caliph, as Egypt was part of the Ottoman Empire at the time. Because of this, my mother's family was considered part of the high aristocracy. They were also wealthy landowners, through land gifted by the Turkish rulers of Egypt. My maternal grandfather, Mohammad Khattab, was a bachelor for the first 35 years of his life, and the events that led to his marriage to my maternal grandmother, a young Austrian woman, flow from two competing familial oral histories.

The first version is that my maternal great-grandfather, a retired Austrian general who was a member of the Imperial Forces, came to Egypt to cure his many ailments at the various fountains and waters, and that he was accompanied by his daughter, who was then 16 or 17 years old. As was customary among aristocracy, the Ottoman Empire's office in Vienna sent a message to the khedive's office in Cairo to receive the retired general appropriately and designate a representative who spoke at least German or French. In the khedive's palace, according to this story, there was a lawyer who happened to be a bachelor and would travel to Europe and also spoke French – and so my grandfather was appointed to do the honours on behalf of the khedive in Egypt. Apparently, this resulted in love at first sight for the general's daughter, and to the chagrin of my grandmother's father, the general, she agreed to marry Mohammad Khattab and stay in Egypt, even though she had no connection to the country, did not speak the language, and without any family or support would have a hard life ahead. The only person who stayed with her was a female attendant, which was quite common in aristocratic families. This woman became the nanny of my maternal grandparents' three children – and then me. I have a few pictures of my nanny and my grandmother, dressed in aristocratic Viennese style.

These pictures form a sharp contrast to the second version of the story, which holds that my Austrian grandmother immigrated to Egypt with her parents from Austria as part of group of Jewish immigrants who fled because of the anti-Jewish pogroms. The story goes that my grandmother was working in Egypt's leading department store, Cicurel, when Mohammad Khattab saw her, fell in love and married her. How she could suddenly become an Austrian aristocrat – as indicated by her style, dress, demeanour and manner of speech as I knew her – is difficult to reconcile.

I have long been confused by these two versions of my ancestor; in the muddle, I go from being a descendant of the Hapsburg aristocracy to being the second generation of a Jewish immigrant family. I once pursued this matter in the 1990s by doing a DNA test, but it proved inconclusive for either theory. As far as I am concerned, I am as comfortable being an Austrian aristocrat as I am being the descendent of Jewish immigrants.

In both versions of the story of my maternal grandparents, after they met and married, they lived in the 27-room house of the Khattab family with my grandmother's Austrian attendant and maintained an Austrian household and way of life. It was in this strict Austrian household that I spent the first years of my life under my grandmother's care, when my parents travelled for my father's diplomatic work. After my grandfather passed away, my grandmother continued to travel to Europe annually, accompanied by one or more of her children, but she always returned to her home and family in Cairo.

I vividly remember how my mother's face would light up when she recounted the deeds of her esteemed father, Mohammad Khattab. He was an attorney who took the brave step of breaking with the aristocracy to support General Ahmed Orabi in his opposition to the British landing at Tel el-Kebir in 1882. My mother used to say that if others had followed in my grandfather's courageous footsteps, Egypt would not have become a nation occupied by the British. My mother, like her father, was a strong-willed individual who blazed her own trail rather than follow the path paved by others.

1946–1955: Cairo

MY FATHER'S WORK for the Ministry of Foreign Affairs continued after the war ended, and by 1946, he was assigned to a post in Brazil. My mother and I did not initially go with him but planned to meet him there after a few months, as my mother had business to attend to in Egypt. That same year, when I was not quite nine years old, my mother went to Alexandria to check on our apartment there, to see what needed to be fixed before summer arrived. While she was away, I stayed in our apartment in the Zamalek district of Cairo. Usta Mohammad Mustafa, our cook, was there, as was a maid who took care of me. My Aunt Perla, the oldest of the three girls and one boy in my mother's family, also came to see me every day.

On one of her visits, Aunt Perla found me listless with a cold. She asked me how long I had had it, and when I told her that my nose had been stuffy for about four days, she took me to an ear, nose and throat specialist who said that I had diphtheria and that if it were not treated quickly, it would spread to my brain and kill me. He told my aunt he did not know how far the diphtheria had progressed and said I might not survive.

My mother rushed back from Alexandria and took me to see a paediatrician, who consulted with the ear, nose and throat specialist and agreed that I needed a massive dose of an anti-diphtheria serum. The problem, they explained to my mother, was that such a large dose would most likely destroy my heart. A cardiologist called in to consult agreed that the proposed dosage would be fatal.

I remember the look on my mother's face as she talked with her sister about the choice ahead: if I got the serum, the diphtheria would stop, but my heart would give up. Without the serum, the diphtheria would kill me.

I don't know how it came to her, but my mother ultimately decided to split the dose in half. Even at half-strength, however, the serum was still strong enough to cause a condition called myocarditis, which could be fatal for someone as young as eight. The children's doctor recommended I have a nurse with me at all times, so I was attended to by an Italian nurse whose husband had been taken prisoner by the British during the war.

The Italian couple lived in Shubra, a suburb of Cairo that at the time was mostly inhabited by Christians, including a large community of Copts, but also middle-income foreigners such as Armenians, Greeks and Italians. Shubra is also the site of a large shrine to Saint Thérèse of Lisieux, a French Catholic who entered a convent in the 1880s when she was 15, died at age 26, and is much admired for the simplicity and practicality of her approach to the spiritual life.

The cardiologist who examined me told my mother that the myocarditis was so severe that I would not survive the night. I remember my mother asking the cardiologist exactly what myocarditis was; as I recall, he said it was basically the breakup of the heart. I later understood that the middle layer of my heart was inflamed, but as an eight-year-old, I faced the incredible prospect that my heart was going to break up and I was going to die.

My Italian nurse left me for a few hours and returned with a little medallion of Saint Thérèse, which she pinned onto my pyjamas just over my heart. One of the side effects of the medication I was taking was that it caused all my glands to swell – the glands under my arms and between my legs were so inflamed and painful that I could not move.

All the doctors agreed that I was not going to live through the night. My mother and a few other people sat with me all night, and from their demeanour and expressions, I really felt as if death were present. I felt as if I were at my own wake.

I don't know exactly how to explain it, but I was not scared. I had a lot of questions, though. Am I going to die? What does that mean? Where am I going to go? Do I come back in some other form? I had all sorts of thoughts that may seem strange for an eight-year-old boy, but none of them was scary to me, and I eventually drifted off to sleep.

The next morning, I woke up alert and hungry. I remember asking for tea and biscuits and help sitting up. Had my glands not been swollen, I probably would have bounded right out of bed. The cardiologist who examined me said he could not believe it, but he found no sign of the myocarditis. I was peppy, playful and cheerful. Everybody said it was a miracle.

My mother pledged to take me to the shrine of Saint Thérèse in Shubra as soon as I was strong enough, and when that happened, I found a huge cathedral with walls covered with little plaques from people who had been cured. Arms and leg braces, dressings and bandages adorned the place. As the Italian nurse well knew, Saint Thérèse had a reputation for healing.

By the end of 1946, I had fully recovered from my illness, and in early 1947, my mother and I went to Brazil to join my father. We stayed there for a year and then all returned to Egypt together.

In February 1949, shortly after I turned 11, my parents divorced. I sided more with my mother. While I bore no sense of animosity toward my father – I always loved him – I did not identify with him. To me, he seemed quiet and laid back, a strong contrast to my mother and her strong personality. My mother knew what she wanted, and she went after it. She was very unconventional in that sense, and could not have cared less what others thought about her and her actions. She smoked, gambled, managed her own money and mingled with high society from all over the world. And she did it all with a sense of grace and confidence. My mother, who was never really impressed with other people, was very much her own woman.

On the other side was my father, a diplomat in career and in personality. Much of what I learned of my father I discovered in the later years of his life, when he started coming to the United States. This is because when I was around 15 years old he became my ward, and I was tasked with managing our family's businesses and affairs.

From my father, I learned that there was wisdom in his form of diplomacy, and by observing him, I learned for myself how to be diplomatic. By this I do not mean the ability to be duplicitous but rather the ability to get your message across in an indirect way, the ability to be tough even though you're smiling, the ability to achieve your mission without really showing your hand.

So my father taught me to be diplomatic, and my mother taught me to be direct. He also taught me how to retreat; my mother, how to advance. I absorbed much from my father, but I always had my mother's temperament, and the two attitudes did not always mesh well together. This could help explain why my parents fought incessantly.

I clearly remember learning about their decision to separate. My parents came into my bedroom, and my mother told me that they were going to divorce and that they wanted me to be present at the divorce. At the time in Egypt, divorce was done by a public official who, if you were wealthy enough, could come to your home to dispense with the matter. The official came to our house with a large book and asked to see the marriage contract. In Islamic marriages, the marriage contract is similar to a prenuptial agreement in that it often provides provisions in the event of divorce: what type of support a spouse should receive, the terms of child custody, any punitive fines resulting from abandonment or infidelity, and other matters. The official executed the terms of my parents' marriage contract. My father agreed that I would live with my mother but that he would pay all my expenses and for our apartment. They discussed visitation, signed their names in the man's enormous book, and then it was over.

At 11 years old, you expect that divorce is going to change everything, that the ceiling will collapse and that the ground will shift beneath you. I waited, but nothing like this happened. My parents tried to guide me through the change. 'Listen, son', my father said, 'I want to tell you one thing: you must always obey and respect your mother.' And he extolled my mother's many virtues.

My mother followed suit, saying that their divorce had nothing to do with me. 'We both love you', she said. 'I respect your father, and he respects me. I don't want to ever hear anything disrespectful of your father while you're living with me.'

This was astonishing, coming from two people who had fought like cats and dogs. I had heard them yelling and screaming at each other all day, and now they were praising each other. I could not make heads or tails of the transformation that had come over them.

But from that day on, I never heard one parent say anything negative about the other – truly, never. And when I was growing up, if I ever tried to raise an issue about one parent with the other, he or she immediately stopped me. 'If that's what your father says', my mother would respond, 'Fine. That's what we'll do.' And vice versa.

I do believe, however, that my father, who was very much in love with my mother, never really recovered from the divorce. He never remarried, never wanted to remarry and to the best of my knowledge never even had a relationship with another woman.

Shortly after the divorce, my father took a post in India. I lived with my mother and attended a Jesuit boarding school. Although I was in turmoil much of my time and did not behave well, I learned important lessons at this Jesuit high school, the College of the Holy Family.

One especially impressive and memorable instructor was Professor Haroun Haddad, an erudite man who taught me Egyptian history, Islamic history and world history, classes in which I did well. Professor Haddad was a member of the nationalist liberal Wafd party who had been an acquaintance and an admirer of my grandfather. In his classes, he reminded students of the epic struggle of Egyptians from all walks of life. Despite my personal struggles at the time, Professor Haddad made a strong impression on me, instilling in me the values of Egypt and Egyptian culture.

But my time at school was troubled. I spent the week at the high school and returned home on the weekends – except when the authorities decided to punish me and keep me at school, which happened often. I became a truly rebellious child. I had no focus. I felt deserted by my parents, that my father taking a post in India and my mother sending me to boarding school were both forms of abandonment. I had no siblings, nobody to talk with about all I had been through in such a short time – my illness and near-death, my family's move to Brazil, our return to Egypt and my parents' divorce – and I became a very difficult child.

By 1950, my father had returned from India, and I chose to live with him for a while. I had become too much for my mother to manage, and she supported my decision, believing it would help ground me.

These years would be a turning point for me, years that pushed me onto a steady, unbending trajectory. Everything went very fast and seemed to point toward a certain, almost predetermined conclusion. I was about to embark on a new beginning; the prologue was wrapping up.

* * *

In 1952, Egypt underwent a revolution in which Gamal Abdel Nasser attained power. It was also the unceremonious end of my father's 25-year diplomatic career. He had risen to the position of director of economic affairs within the Ministry of Foreign Affairs, a position equivalent to assistant secretary of state in the United States, but the Nasser regime summarily forced him out because he belonged to a prominent Wafdist family, and Nasser wanted no rivals as he clamped down on power. Two of my uncles, one of whom was in the foreign service and one of whom was in the military, were also forced out as part of this escalating purge. My uncles ultimately filed suit with the Council of State and, after 20 years, they prevailed and received compensation as well as retirement at the rank they would have obtained had they not been removed from service.

My father was given the choice of reassignment, which amounted to a demotion, or dismissal. He had thought that he would be exempt from the purge because of his qualifications and reputation for being completely apolitical, and after decades of service, he took the news of his dismissal or reassignment very badly. He became severely depressed and suffered a total collapse, debilitating enough that he could no longer take care of himself or the family's affairs. And so when I was 15, my father became my ward. With no experience in such things, I assumed responsibility for the household, my father's care and running 250 acres of farmland in the Nile Delta.

***

In 1953, when I was in my second year of high school, I decided to accelerate my education by sitting for a comprehensive high school examination in 1955. I was eager to join the Military Academy and become an officer, and this move would have allowed me to finish high school two years early. Against my father's wishes, I stayed home from school for an entire year to study for the exam while also managing to care for my father and my family's affairs. It was a valuable lesson for me: I had my father, my family and our farms to care for, and a future military career and family waiting for me. I learned how to juggle, how to prioritise and how to be responsible. I didn't have time to rebel anymore.

During this time, I became very close with one of my family's trusted circle, Haj Abdul Hamid. Haj Abdul Hamid, who first worked for my maternal grandfather, then for my mother, then my father and finally me, provided the guidance I needed to handle the burdens this excitable 15-year-old had just inherited. He also served as a mentor. When I was placed under house arrest a few years later, it was Haj Abdul Hamid who visited me and kept me from the hazards of isolation. I have always thought of him with great fondness.

When I was 15, my dream was to become an officer, get married, have children and have a nice, stable life. I wanted everything that I missed as a child. Nothing could stop me or even slow me down. By age 17, I not only had my Egyptian secondary education diploma but I had earned the French baccalaureate, which allowed me to obtain a scholarship to the University of Dijon. My father had been opposed to my going to the Military Academy, and when I found out that 1955 would be the last year in which it would be possible to complete a legal education in France in three years instead of the customary four, the choice for me was clear. I was not about to waste any time as I barrelled toward the future of national service in the model of my forebears. I believed that I had been well instructed by my mentors and that my mettle had been tested.

***

Sheikh Hassan el-Sayed was a high school teacher and graduate of the Al-Azhar University. At the tail end of my rebellious adolescent phase, he tutored me from the age of 14 at home in Arabic and religion twice a week, as was traditional in families such as ours. Through Sheikh Hassan, I learned a great deal about the spirituality of Islam. He introduced me to a Sufi school at Al Hussein Mosque, and every Thursday evening he and I would go with some other friends and participate in prayer and Sufi rituals. Sheikh Hassan was very secular in his appearance, and for the three years that he was my teacher, he was the most influential person in my life.

One day, when Sheikh Hassan arrived for my private lessons wearing his usual sandals and bright white, perfectly pressed shirt, I quickly noticed a cut on the heel of his foot that was swelling badly. I urged him to go to the doctor, but he refused. When I pleaded with him to let me take him to get care, he was unmoved, insisting that he would just go to the public hospital. This frustrated me immensely, as much because of what I considered Sheikh Hassan's unnecessary frugality as my concern for his health. In all the time I studied with him, he was so tightfisted, so parsimonious, that when I had a lesson around lunchtime, I often found that he had nothing to eat. I had no problem asking Usta Mohammad Mustafa, our cook, to bring him a plate of food or fruit, perhaps with some bread and cheese, but that wasn't the point. What bothered me was that he was so cheap he wouldn't even buy himself a sandwich. Sometimes, when I asked him why he was late for one of our sessions, he would explain that the public transportation had been late. 'For God's sake', I would tell him, 'You're making a lot of money from private lessons. Get a taxi!' I just didn't understand why a man who earned a good living was so stingy.

Yet that day I finally was able to persuade Sheikh Hassan to let my father's driver take him and me to the public hospital. Doctors drained the swelling in his foot, but the infection was a serious one, and the next time I saw him, his foot looked even worse. This time I drove him to the hospital, where the doctors said the foot was gangrenous and had to come off. I wanted to take him to the private hospital, but he refused. I was furious with him. 'But I'll pay for it!' I pleaded.

Sheikh Hassan was adamant, and his foot was amputated just above the ankle at the public hospital. When we learned that the gangrene had spread and he was in very bad shape, however, he finally agreed to let me take him to a private hospital. I carried him in my arms, put him in the back of the car and drove him to the hospital, where my family connections were such that I was able to get doctors to treat him at no charge. The doctors found that his gangrene had continued to spread, and even after amputating the leg at the knee, they were not certain that he would live. I could see that he was suffering.

At one point, when we were alone, Sheikh Hassan pulled out a Qur'an.

'I want you to swear on this Qur'an that what I'm about to tell you, you will keep secret', he said, speaking carefully. I agreed.

'Here's a power of attorney', he said. 'You must go to my high school and withdraw my salary. Take half of it, go to my house, and give it to my wife. Don't tell her about the other half. With the other half of the money, here is a list of people whom you go to.'

He proceeded to tell me about five families he was caring for. For one, I was to buy their groceries. For another, I was to give them money. And so it went.

I then realised that he was tightfisted because he was supporting his own family and five others as a work of charity. He was so humble that he didn't tell anyone, not even his own wife. And he wanted no recognition or thanks.

'Please, please', he said, 'When you do the shopping for this family and give them the bag, just leave it near the door. Don't even hand it to them. And give them my apologies. Tell them "Haj Hassan sends you this, and apologises that he can't come."' Then he added, 'And please apologise for how little there is in the bag.'

Unfortunately, Sheikh Hassan's condition worsened, and he died shortly afterward. I carried him out of the hospital, put him into my car, and drove him to his house, where his family gathered around him before the mortician arrived. The family said a common prayer before the mortician took Sheikh Hassan's body to the mosque for a communal prayer and then burial in a white linen shroud.

The final weeks of Sheikh Hassan's life showed me what a man of humility and faith he was and all that he did for others. He taught me to think, he taught me to live by my beliefs, and in those last weeks, he taught me about true selflessness and giving. These were the lessons from Sheikh Hassan that I carried with me on my next journey and all those that followed.

August 1955: Dijon, France

I STOOD ALONE on the train platform, surrounded by my four oversized suitcases, packed to the brim at the insistence of my parents. It was August 1955, and I had just arrived in Dijon, France. After wrestling the luggage off the train and onto the platform, I stopped to catch my breath and decide on a course of action. Finally I spotted a lonely porter, and although he dealt only with commercial packages, he took pity on me and brought me a wagon for my suitcases.

After learning that I had booked a room at the Hotel de la Cloche, which was only about a hundred metres from the train station, the porter was kind enough to show me the way. I have no clue what I would have done without his help: I could carry only two suitcases at a time, and I could not leave the others unattended.

This was the first, small sign that things were going to be different in France and that without my family and their many employees to help me, I would have to deal with challenges on my own.

I thought I had been forced to become an adult overnight a mere two years before, when I had taken over my family's business after my father's psychological collapse. But I soon realised that with my affluent background and considerable support from those around me, I was still more privileged than most. I had become the person on whom 12 farmers and their families depended for housing, food, water and work, and in that new position people respected me and accepted my authority. But I did not have to earn it.

In my new life in Dijon, I was alone and vulnerable in an unknown world, and I would need to work hard to find my place. I had lost the safety net I had enjoyed all my life: if something horrible happened, I would not know whom to call, where to go, or what to do.

The turmoil of being unmoored by a shift from one universe to another, which I experienced many times in my life, highlighted the significance of small things and heightened my sense of appreciation of God. In a sense, it seems that God has always tested me, putting me in some of the worst positions and then steering me out of them into much better ones. At the time I arrived in Dijon at 17½ years old, I was at a low place in my life.

When I found the listing of places for students to live at the student centre, I decided to rent a room by myself, not knowing that to save money most students chose to share a room. I had a small scholarship for that first year – 40 French francs a month – so sharing accommodation would have made financial sense, but it was not an option I even considered. I had never shared a room before. I was also at least two years younger than almost everyone in my class.

It didn't take me long to realize that 40 francs was only enough to live on for about 15 days, so I had to scurry and find a job somewhere to make ends meet. I found work as a dishwasher at a local restaurant and then as a bottle-washer and filler/corker for a seller of cheap burgundy wines.

More than half of my freshman class of 120 students had government scholarships. The students were primarily from working-class families, and most were excellent in their work and very determined. I was one of a small number of foreigners there and one of the very few Arab Muslims, which many other students found quite exotic. But it was 1955, a time when the Algerian revolution against France was starting, and Algerians and Arabs were viewed with a kind of enmity, somewhat similar to the Islamophobia in the present-day United States, and I was viewed with some hostility. I could sense that a segment of my class was right-wing, racist and looked down on me.

I had gone from an aristocratic position to one where I was treated with prejudice and contempt, and once again the contrast was like a cold shower. But it also taught me what racism really means – and how it feels to be part of a downtrodden caste.

I also had to traverse a cultural gulf. In Egypt I had studied in a French Jesuit school, but this was not the same as being brought up in France, and I had to work twice as hard as my classmates to stay at the top level of the class.

I had a number of clashes with some of the right-wingers, who were always making nasty remarks. The entrance to the law school, an 18th-century building, was like that of a castle. Walking to class, students would stand on the sides and smoke, and often they would look askance at me and make snide comments. It took all my self-control not to start a fight with those making degrading remarks, and in a few instances, classmates who understood where I was coming from stood in the way and prevented it from boiling over. The environment at my Jesuit school in Egypt had been very disciplined, and I had never had such encounters before; in my book, these other students were thugs, but I came to the realisation that the only way I could shut them up was by being better than they were in our studies.

I felt like I was a kid, churlish and ill at ease. I tried to grow a mustache, but it was very sparse, and one of the racist kids took note, saying something to the effect that Arabs had so many failings that they did not even have enough hair to grow a mustache. I was very upset, and on my way home that day I saw a tobacco store. I had never smoked in my life, but I saw a pipe and bought it.

Thus, before the age of 18, I started munching on the pipe, although I did not smoke it and never intended to. I looked at myself in the mirror and I convinced myself that I looked a bit older. I would sit at the café in the student centre and put the pipe in my mouth, even though everyone knew I did not smoke. I struck a pose like this until one of my friends bought a little pouch of tobacco, filled the pipe, stuck the pipe in my mouth and lit it up for me. I almost choked to death smoking that first pipe, but from then on, I smoked for fifty years – until I had my first heart attack and the doctor told me I could not smoke anymore. But at the time, as the days passed in Dijon, pipe smoking was a signal of my adulthood.

I soon joined what was termed the Radical Party in France, and the anticolonial movement, both of which were burgeoning across campuses and cities. There were constant demonstrations against the xenophobic and racist French who kept saying that Algeria was French and had to remain French. We were pelted and insulted, and both citizens and the police were rough with us. It was in these moments that I learned to be an activist. I was also a member of the Arab Students' Organisation, although there were only six Arab students across Dijon's faculties, so the local group did not amount to much. The anticolonial movement was mostly made up of north Africans, people from the French African colonies. There were also a lot of French liberals akin to those drawn to the civil rights movement in United States in the 1960s. It was more of an activist or rights movement than anything else, but the ideas and composition were the same.

Generally, at least at first, I was a fish out of water when it came to social norms. By this, I mean that I had no idea how to deal with women. Between my Jesuit studies and a fairly conventional traditional Islamic family upbringing, I was taught very early on about all the sexual taboos that have since then become both unremarkable and part of everyday life. The Jesuits were particularly rigid. For example, we could not put our arms under the bedcovers, even in winter when it was almost freezing, nor could we put our hands in our trouser pockets because this suggested masturbation, which was still a grave sin for Catholics. It was also a big sin among Muslims.

From both sides, I was taught not to stare at women, not to steal a look at any part of their bodies, and to avoid being sexually aroused. Touching or kissing a woman was not only a religious but a social taboo. By the time I left for France as a law student, I had held hands with a girl only a few times at a movie, in the dim light of the theatre. That was the extent of my sexual experience.

When I got to France, even though I had travelled to Europe with my parents several times, I found myself struck by the number of beautiful and attractive women at the university, mostly in the school of liberal arts. (The law school had only a handful of women, who seemed to have been selected on the basis of their unappealing looks.) Some classmates finally persuaded me to go out with them on a Saturday evening to a place that had music and dancing, but because I didn't drink, I just sat there like a bump on a log.

The following Saturday, a girl from liberal arts came and sat next to me in the student café, most likely because she took pity on me. We spent the evening talking. I was thoroughly clumsy, speaking mostly about myself, my family and Egypt. We saw each other a few times and advanced to holding hands and kissing on the cheek when we parted company.

Then one day, a classmate asked me what the problem was between me and the girl. Apparently she had approached the only other Egyptian student at Dijon and sought his advice. 'Well, I really like Cherif very much', she said, 'but there is something wrong with him.' And she told him that I wouldn't make a move on her.

'You know, she's complaining about you', the classmate told me.

In my surprise, I asked what she could possibly be complaining about.

'She said that all you do is kiss her on the cheek.'

'And what else am I supposed to do?', I asked him.

'You don't know what you're supposed to do?' He was incredulous. 'Hasn't anybody taught you?' His insinuation shocked me, and I said that such a thing couldn't be done if this girl and I were not getting married. He looked at me intensely, nodded, and left. I never saw the female student from the school of liberal arts again.

This produced a crisis of ego that led to introspection, and maybe because of my legalistic mind I sought a rationale. I came up with the proposition that all the rules in Islam were applicable to a Muslim society, within a Muslim country, and since I was outside a Muslim society, I could adopt these new customs and mores and not necessarily be bound by Islamic law. This rationale never sat too easily with me, but three months later I acted on it, and by the end of my time at Dijon, after almost two years in a French university, a place where sex is positively commonplace, I had had two such encounters, which gave me as much guilt as pleasure.

Despite day-to-day exasperations, I finished my first year of courses fifth in my class in written exams and ninth in oral exams. I surprised many when I decided to sit for the national competition on French civil law. To everyone's astonishment, including my own, I received second place in that competition, which no foreigner or first-year law student had ever won before.

With fairer wind in my sails, I could not wait for my second and third years of law school. In short order, I imagined, I would be back in Egypt and on my way to following in both my grandfathers' footsteps. One had been a populist criminal defence attorney, and the other an aristocratic attorney belonging to the Royal Court. The complexities and contradictions of their paths would prepare me to play many roles throughout my career.

July–December 1956:
Dijon, Alexandria and Cairo

O N 26 JULY 1956, Egyptian President Gamal Abdel Nasser announced that he would nationalise the Suez Canal. In response, France and the United Kingdom, shareholders of the Suez Canal Company since its construction in 1869, threatened to invade Egypt and urged Israel to join them.

I saw my country on the brink of recolonisation, and I believed that this was my time to act, just as my predecessors had when it was their time. I was both proudly nationalistic and deeply concerned. I had attended meetings of the Arab Students' Organisation in Paris and worked with students from north and sub-Saharan Africa, students who were fighting for independence and would eventually return to their countries to continue the struggle. We all had declared our firm belief in the principle of self-determination.

In working with the Arab Students' Organisation, however, I also thought I understood exactly why we Arabs were in such a predicament. Hearing so many Arab students shouting, as if to debate, was the most disheartening experience I'd ever had. I'll never forget how vociferous and argumentative some of the students were. They were so confrontational, constantly going back and forth, amplifying the discourse, accusing each other, and polemicising incessantly. I thought that at any moment things would erupt and people would end up in fisticuffs. In the end, it was just a series of speeches, each speaker waiting for the moment he or she could interject and out-talk the other. I found this especially distasteful because, as I saw it, Egypt was on the verge of being recolonised. Arabism and its supporters needed to step up, but they were crumbling, too busy heedlessly pecking at each other. I realised quickly that most of the participants in these gatherings, who came from all over France and were representing almost every Arab country, were disorganised, impractical, undisciplined and primarily preoccupied with prestige, with being seen as the meeting's most important leader.

Dismayed by the students' behaviour and fearful about what was happening in Egypt, I decided to postpone my studies and return home to enlist in the army. I believed I was witnessing the end of Arab nationalism and that the Arab world, starting with Egypt, was going to get pulled back under the heel of imperialists. Although I never thought that I, as just one person, could change this, I nevertheless wanted to stand up against these antagonists in the most active way possible. If my country was going to be undone, I was going to go down with it. It was a decision that came easily to me.

When I told the other students in the organisation about my plan, most of them tried to talk me out of it. Why, they wondered, would I want to leave France? But in the end, they were generous enough to help me buy my return ticket.

As a scholarship student, I had very little money and was able to purchase only an 'on-deck' ticket, which gave me one chaise longue to sleep on for the passage. As a parting gift, one of my Egyptian class-mates gave me a blanket so that I could keep warm on the boat. I said my goodbyes, took the train to Marseille, bought myself some food for the trip, and was off.

When I landed in Alexandria in August 1956, my father, who had moved there, met me at the dock. Although my father completely opposed my plan to enlist, he was always gentle and never tried to impose his view on me. I had proven myself by taking over as head of our household before going to France, so I had earned a certain level of respect from the man. I continued on to Cairo, where I stayed in our apartment alone, as my mother was travelling at the time.

The next morning, I went to the Cairo office of my second cousin, Major General Abdel Moneim Riad, who was the head of field artillery. I had always been fond of him because he treated me like a kid brother. General Riad was known as a soldier's soldier, a man of discipline. He had grown up in a military family, and after his father died at an early age, he was brought up by his mother and stepfather, Taher el-Kholy, who was my aunt's husband, and he was at my family's house often.

That day he did not take my news well.

'Are you crazy?', he screamed at me, in typical Egyptian fashion. 'You left your studies in France to come here? Do you think this country needs more soldiers?'

There was no cause to have left school early, he lectured me, and because I had not been to the Military Academy I could not hope to be anything more than a grunt.

He ordered me to take the next plane or boat back to France and threatened to call my father to make sure I resumed my studies. He then turned to his chief of staff, a colonel, and told him to find someone to take me home immediately. The colonel directed me to a captain, who drove me home. The trip between the neighbourhoods of Abbasiya and Garden City was a long one, and the young captain, who eventually rose to the positions of chief of staff of the armed forces and minister of defence, became my friend.

I spent the next day moping around, utterly deflated. I took a walk and was trying to clear my thoughts and figure out what to do next when someone in uniform pulled up next to me on a motorcycle.

'Cherif?', he asked.

The motorcyclist turned out to be a man from the neighbourhood whom I had not seen in two years.

After I told him of my thwarted plans, he invited me to hop onto his motorcycle. I noticed his uniform: instead of the officer's insignia on the shoulders (a single star for a second lieutenant and two stars for a first), his had two golden stripes. The badge of his beret had the usual infantry insignia, but in the middle of the eagle, the symbol of Egypt, there was a skull and crossbones against a red background, which, he explained, was the emblem of the Fedayeen in the National Guard. This unit, I came to learn, had been developed in 1954, and its role was essentially to undertake guerilla incursions into Israel from Gaza. One regiment was staged in Gaza, and another regiment was deployed later at the bottom of the Sinai, near what is now Sharm el-Sheikh.[4]

We drove back to Abbaysia, where just the day before I had been rebuked by General Riad, but sped past the military buildings and barracks to get to the headquarters of the National Guard (*al-Haras al-Watani*). My companion led me into the command structure building, up to the first floor into what appeared to be the office of the commander, General Ahmed Anwar.

My young neighbour worked on General Anwar's staff. In response to the general's questions, I confirmed that I was related to General Riad and to Mahmoud Bassiouni Pasha (an honorary title dating from the time when Egypt had been under the Ottoman Empire, a title that survived until 1953, when the Revolutionary Command Council abolished it), my paternal grandfather. He asked if I had really left my studies in France to volunteer to defend my country, and for a third time I answered in the affirmative.

---

[4] The Fedayeen fought alongside Palestinian volunteers under the then-leadership of Yasser Arafat, who after the 1993 Oslo Agreement became the first President of the Palestinian Authority. He was also the founder and head of the Fatah movement (the Palestinian National Liberation Movement, *Harakat al-Tahrir al-Watani al-Filastini*), and ultimately won the Nobel Peace Prize, along with Israeli leaders Yitzhak Rabin and Shimon Peres.

After only a few more questions, the general told his chief of staff to enrol me in the officers' candidate school for the Fedayeen of the National Guard, akin to the US Special Forces. In one hour, I had gone from a reject to a member of what was reputed to be an elite military unit. And so began my short-lived military career, one day after I thought it would never start.

I felt unstoppable, sure that in no time I would have those gold stripes on my shoulders. But as I later learned, the one-year programme for becoming an officer in the Fedayeen was not the same as the Military Academy's four-year programme. Moreover, by then, because of the possibility of imminent attack by Britain, France and Israel, the Fedayeen's one-year officer programme had been shortened to three months. I believed I could use the position I would earn through the accelerated programme, something slightly less than a second lieutenant in the army, to find a way around it and have a regular army career, but the most I could ever earn through the army would be two gold stripes. I would deal with all of that later, I thought in my urgency. I was in, and nothing, not even reason, was going to ruin that for me.

1930s, 1956: Cairo

FOR THE ENTIRE motorcycle ride back to Garden City, I was adrift with elation, my imagination reeling over the prospects of my military refashioning. I returned to reality only after getting dropped off at my apartment building and being told by my friend that I should report for duty the next morning at 0700 at what used to be the agricultural fairgrounds, just across the Qasr el-Nil bridge, not very far from where I lived. (Today, these grounds are the seat of the Cairo Opera House, still surrounded by gardens.)

All night, my mind was awash with thoughts about how I would live up to the legacies of my grandfathers. I thought of my paternal grandfather, Mahmoud Bassiouni, who despite serving on the Egyptian Senate, was known for his humility and sensitivity toward others.

As I tried to sleep, a story about my grandfather at the inauguration of those same fairgrounds where I would be reporting the next morning reverberated in my head. This tale was told to me by Usta Mohammad Mustafa, our cook, when I was five years old, and it quickly became my favourite bedtime story.

According to the story, the dignitaries at the inauguration ceremony included King Fuad, who led the procession, the prime minister, and my grandfather, who looked on in the line nearby. At some point, during all the pomp and circumstance, Mahmoud Bassiouni caught a glimpse of the son of a dear old friend.

He reached across the prime minister and rather unceremoniously tapped the arm of the king to grab his attention. After telling the prime minister to ask the king to excuse him for a few minutes, my grandfather peeled off to the right of the procession, zipped past the soldiers standing at attention, and went straight to the young conscript, whom he addressed as 'Ibn Steta', meaning 'son of Steta'.

Steta, the old friend, was a widow with four children who delivered milk to my grandfather's home every morning in Asyut. My grandfather was so grateful to Steta that each day when she arrived, he would personally thank and pay her. He made sure that everyone in the household knew that they should be grateful to Steta for her sacrifice, for coming in early every morning just after morning prayers, walking two miles each way, to make a living for her children. This kind of genuine caring is what made my grandfather a beloved figure in Upper Egypt. To Mahmoud Bassiouni, every human being was special and deserved to be treated with the dignity that he believed God created and bestowed on all mankind.

My grandfather returned to a confused king and his entourage and supposedly said, 'My apologies, your majesty, but that was the son of Steta, who for years, winter and summer, would bring milk every morning by sunrise for my children.' And so my grandfather, who interrupted the procession, forced the king and all his high-level dignitaries to stop and wait so that he could say hello to a young conscript (who, needless to say, was stunned by all the attention). Upon hearing my grandfather's explanation, the king reportedly clapped his hands in amazement and said loudly, 'Only Mahmoud Bassiouni can get away with something like this.' The others laughed, some probably in jealous dismay, others supposedly in amazement.

A few minutes later, the story goes, the prime minister asked my grandfather what had possessed him to break rank in such a way.

My grandfather's answer was simple. 'Could you imagine if he went back home and told Steta that Mahmoud Bassiouni passed in front of him without greeting him, after all she did for my children for all of those years? She would be devastated.'

As I walked down the slopes of the agricultural gardens the next morning, I reviewed the story in my mind, trying to imagine how it might have played out. I wondered where my grandfather was at each turn of the story, where the young conscript stood in shock as my grandfather made his way over to him, and what the expressions had been on the faces of the dignitaries who looked on.

* * *

I made my way into the wooden shack on the grounds where my military career would begin. At the front desk, I was told that they had received a phone call about me but since there were no written orders, nobody would stop me from starting my training. I was directed to a supply shed where I was issued my field uniform, two pairs of khakis, two pairs of shirts and only one pair of shoes. I looked at the size 13 boots, which were two sizes too big, and then noticed that the tip of both shoes went slightly to the right. I went to the sergeant and told him that not only did the boots not fit – they were both right boots.

'Soldier', he retorted, 'I receive boots in pairs. I gave you a pair. If you have two rights, it means that out there, somewhere, there is a soldier with two lefts.'

He then followed with, 'You go out there, and you look for the soldier with two lefts. Trade one of your rights for one of his lefts, and if the boots are too big for you, then wear two pairs of socks. Next!'

As I looked at my oversized, mismatched boots, my expectations of glorious military life began to fade. I wore the shoes with the persistence, or perhaps the stubbornness, that is characteristic of people from Upper Egypt. I wore the shoes all throughout basic training, even though my superiors and fellow officers made fun of me in training. It was not until I finished basic training three weeks later, when I was transferred to the western Cairo command, that I was finally able to go to a military surplus store to buy a new pair of boots.

On this first day of training, my world, that of an aristocratic, privileged, wealthy young man, was again upturned. I found myself among the poor and downtrodden, rural people from a lower class, many of whom were illiterate, and often went to bed hungry. I saw officers treat conscripts as though they truly were subhuman. They called them dirty names, and hit and kicked them. The non-commissioned officers had a different attitude toward the men because they probably came from similar backgrounds, but they still treated the men as objects, like pieces of equipment. To them, the men were not subhuman and yet were not truly human, either. They were treated as robots, expected to walk straight when the order came to walk straight, to turn left when it came to turn left.

I think the word had spread that I was going to an officer's training school and that I came from the upper class, so the officers all treated me relatively politely. I did not make too many mistakes, luckily, but once in a while the order would come to face right and I would turn left and I would be yelled at, but not with the terrible names and humiliating insults that were hurled at the others. This had a striking effect on me, and I remember it hurt me profoundly. I tried to share this with a few of the officers, but I realised that I was speaking to people who had come from an entirely different frame of reference.

Later, when I was commissioned and had my own unit, I was so conscious of these things that I always ate the same thing the conscripts did and never ordered outside food in the presence of enlisted men unless I ordered enough for the entire unit. I refused to act as the other officers did.

I was certainly as militaristic and domineering as any other young officer would be, but that was because I was only 18, almost 19, and my background made me accustomed to ordering people around. I can only hope that I was not demeaning to others, but this class differential and the distinction between officers and men, this lack of respect for one's human dignity, left a mark on me, and I would keep seeing it. Even as late as 2016, Egyptian officers routinely insulted and beat conscripts.[5]

The National Guard, which had been established under Nasser, was an institution designed to spite the military establishment. It consisted mostly of people who believed in the Nasser ideals of the revolution and were not only nationalistic but veering socialist. This was very new to the Arab Muslim world because it was a secular movement, and it separated the religious from the secular. Nasserist socialist tendencies were influenced by Marx more than anything else. Emerging institutions such as the National Guard and the Arab Socialist Party were transformed when members from the working class joined.

Soon people from the upper classes would be rare; someone such as myself, coming from an aristocratic family, would be probably 1 in 1,000. The majority of members were from the lower class, with a good number of people from the middle class.

Socialism had strong appeal, particularly for those in the lower classes. These men brought with them a particular culture, and even though I was not a classical or traditional aristocrat who was accustomed to looking down on others and was respectful of my fellow human beings, to them I was still an outsider. If I sat with my men or with my fellow officers for a meal, even the way we ate was different. We all ate with our hands – nobody ate with utensils – but perhaps I was more uppity than others in my mannerisms.

'What, is he afraid of dirtying his hands and putting his fingers in the sauce? He's sort of a delicate dandy', they seemed to say. The same was true of how I would sit or talk in comparison to my men, who conducted themselves in a manner much different from what I knew.

At the beginning I was looked upon with a great deal of suspicion. People saw that I tried very hard, but still they made life a little difficult for me, prodding me to prove myself all the time. This difficult time, a sort of hazing, is typical of Egypt's very class-conscious society.

The National Guard was also regarded as the poor brother of the Army. It was set apart, not like its counterpart in the United States or other countries, where the National Guard can be part of the

---

military mainstream. Regular Army officers did not recognise officers in the National Guard on the grounds that National Guard members had not attended the Military Academy. These distinctions caused much friction between officers in the National Guard and officers in the Army, exacerbated by class tensions.

The strains were further amplified between the National Guard and the Army as a result of the special unit, the Fedayeen. In 1956, when the war with French, British and Israeli forces began over the nationalisation of the Suez Canal, and I enlisted, the Fedayeen were in Gaza, halfway between the border of Israel and the Sinai. The two small brigades, *katibas*, which each consisted of somewhere between 1,000 and 1,100 men, fiercely distinguished themselves. And it was there that I found myself after a mere three weeks of basic training and a few weeks at a western Cairo command post, where I had been subsequently stationed. Still so green, I was dispatched to lay mines and explosives outside of Port Said, which was then the first line of defence against the French and the British.

On 7 November 1956, in the eight final hours before the implementation by all parties of UN General Assembly resolution 997 calling for a ceasefire, our Fedayeen unit was the only thing standing between the might of the French and British and the Egyptian forces. I was in command of a brigade of 70 men, and we were bombarded and shelled for those eight hours. Fifty-six of these men died around me, and the rest of us were wounded. I received four shrapnel wounds in my right leg, although these were not severe. Later, I would receive the highest medal for valour from President Nasser, who, in his infinite wisdom, decided that our small unit, not the UN brokered ceasefire, had stopped the British and French advance. Afterward, I was assigned to a training camp in Cairo while I recovered from my wounds.

In the aftermath of Port Said, Nasser decided to get rid of all his senior officers, including many at the rank of colonel, but he was concerned about creating dissatisfaction within the ranks of the military and thus did not quite know what to do with these dismissed officers. This was the same period in which Nasser had decided to kick all the French and British citizens residing in Egypt, as well as all the Egyptian Jews, out of the country. He did this by sequestering and then nationalising all their assets, denying them any form of income. Nationalising all these assets and making a number of private companies into national ones turned out to be an unintentional short-term solution to his problem of dismissed officers, as the officers he had dismissed from the military were assigned to be the managers of these companies. Suddenly a chocolate or cigarette factory, a factory that belonged to an Egyptian Jew whose family had been in Egypt for 300 years, was taken over. The owner was kicked out of his homeland, and his factory was turned over to a former army general, who, of course, knew little or nothing about running a business.

Nasser's decision in 1956 to overhaul the economy set into motion a sequence of events the impact of which can still be felt in Egypt today. With this move, a substantial segment of the national economy was transferred to the public sector, satisfying the administration's socialist ideals. But in addition to dispossessing so many people of their property and livelihood, it inadvertently began the legacy of cronyism and corruption that would culminate in the collapse of the Egyptian government in 2011. The dismissed military officers now heading Egyptian companies were sheltered from trying to keep afloat in a typical market system, and they were salaried. As the nationalised economy and public sector economy expanded, the private sector became smaller and competitive forces were dampened.

Management of these companies was atrocious. The dismissed officers-turned-CEOs were not only completely inept; they tended to appoint their sons, sons-in-laws, brothers and cousins to important managerial positions. This cronyism and corruption carried over from Nasser to Anwar Sadat to Hosni Mubarak.

To rehabilitate the Egyptian army, Nasser chose my cousin, General Abdel Moneim Riad, to be chief of staff. Nasser knew Riad well because they had been classmates in the Military Academy. General Riad took the job under one condition: that Nasser would give him carte blanche to revamp the military. Nasser agreed. What he was able to achieve was exceptional, which was why Egypt was able to partially win the war against Israel in October 1973.

General Riad's major reforms included reorganising the officer class into three categories to foster specialisation of skills, overhauling training programmes, and initiating the strategy of putting the Egyptian forces along the Suez Canal. Although my appetite for military history persisted throughout my life, General Raid's reforms did not involve me. By that time, I was building a new life for myself in the United States.

December 1956: Cairo

THE MONTH FOLLOWING the battle of Port Said, in December 1956, after retreating from the Sinai and recovering from my injury, I was assigned to a camp in downtown Cairo, part of a paramilitary organisation referred to as the Civil Defence by the military. As well as the local police, the force consisted of volunteers organised on the basis of police districts in the cities of Cairo and Ismailia and Suez along the canal. The military assigned the Civil Defence to carry out guerilla warfare against any foreign occupation, assuming that France, Britain or Israel might continue their plan to occupy the rest of Egypt. The Egyptian military knew that such a defeat would be precipitated by the loss of Ismailia at the centre of the canal and Suez at the south.

1993: The Former Yugoslavia

WE FIRST HEARD reports of a mass grave with as many as 1,700 bodies at Pakračka Poljana in Croatia – and that local Serbs had reported a large number of missing persons in the area – during a reconnaissance mission in early 1993.

Getting to the site took time, but by October 1993 we finally had the necessary approval of local officials and a team from Ovčara to assist in the search. After digging out 17 trenches at the site, each about 10 metres long and 2 metres wide, however, we found no mass grave. Further excavations of 71 areas in the vicinity uncovered nothing.

A team of Dutch specialists, convinced that so many reports of missing Serbs must have merit, finally uncovered 19 bodies buried close together in Pakračka Poljana and determined that the individuals, who were buried in nine separate graves, had all been executed. Despite plans made in advance, Krajina Serb officials refused to allow the bodies to be moved to Croatia for autopsy.

Winter was settling in, and our fieldwork had to stop. Because Pakračka Poljana had no facilities for proper post-mortem examinations, we were forced to place the bodies in body bags and rebury them at a place controlled by members of the UN Protection Force.

The open field where the bodies were reburied was surrounded by woods, and the closest hamlet was about 20 kilometres away. As I stood in the field watching the bodies be prepared for reburial, I thought of my apartment and elegant offices at UN Headquarters in Geneva, which were befitting for an assistant secretary-general, which was my position at the time. I could have stayed in the comforts of Geneva, but instead I chose to sleep on a cot under a tent, just as the Dutch military did. That winter was a particularly cold one, and the Dutch unit had no hot water and only two portable toilets for almost 90 people. But I knew that unlike those who lay just feet from me, who had suffered untimely and certainly unceremonious deaths, I had chosen to be there, to do all I could for the work of the commission.

One of the 19 bodies was that of a middle-aged woman who had been wrapped in a blanket and whose hands, folded over her chest, held her shoes and hat. She had clearly been killed elsewhere, wrapped in the blanket, moved, and then dumped in the grave. She wore a long white dress that came down to her ankles, and there was something angelic about her. Something about the woman – and the stark reburial scene – made me want to mark the occasion.

I knew that a Jordanian peacekeeping force of about 400 men was stationed about 8 kilometres away, so I drove to its headquarters, met with the commanding officer, a brigadier general from Special Forces, and asked whether some of his soldiers could dig individual graves for the bodies we had found. He readily agreed, and the soldiers dug nineteen graves side by side.

We had no idea who the nineteen dead were and no way of finding out. Without thinking much about it, I asked the Jordanian lieutenant commanding the detail whether his men could make Serb Orthodox crosses to mark the graves. When the lieutenant responded with a startled look, I thought perhaps he did not know that the Serb Orthodox cross has a second, smaller crossbar above the conventional bar used by other Christians, but I quickly realized, with something approaching amusement, that he was a Muslim Bedouin Jordanian who had probably never even heard of a Serb Orthodox cross – and that he must think it very strange that such a request was coming from me, another Muslim who was also an Arab. When the Jordanian soldiers, without hesitation or complaint, buried and built crosses for unknown Orthodox Serbs, people who were known to kill Bosnian Muslims, I was overwhelmed with respect and affection for the commander and for his men.

The Jordanians finished digging, transferred the dead into the 19 individual graves, covered the bodies with earth, planted the Orthodox markers, and put up a small fence around the gravesite. When it was all done, the Dutch military unit assigned to the Commission of Experts for the mass grave exhumations (which we affectionately called the Gravediggers Platoon), the team of forensic experts and the Jordanian soldiers all gathered at the gravesite.

The Jordanians were the only ones armed with rifles, and their lieutenant called them to attention. Then the Dutch lieutenant colonel did the same. It was one of the most moving experiences of my life – so natural, so human, so poignant, so real – and a symbol of our common humanity. We all stood in silence, paying our respects to unknown brothers and sisters killed in what must have been terrible circumstances. We came from different parts of the world and held different religious beliefs, but we were united in our common human bond and, I daresay, our belief in God.

None of us was in a hurry to disband, and all were hushed. Most had their gaze to the ground. Few made eye contact, and for a while no one spoke. Then the Jordanians bade me farewell and left, and I strolled to the Dutch tent, passing the wooden sign put up by someone in the Dutch unit that said 'The Gravediggers Platoon'.

That evening, I attended a traditional Jordanian feast in my honour given by the Jordanian commander. The brigadier general had ordered the slaughter of a sheep, which was cooked on a spit over an open fire and put on a mound of rice in a traditional Bedouin meal called *mansaf*. We ate standing at an elevated table, warmed by nearby field fires, and in keeping with Jordanian tradition, I joined the officers in eating with the fingers of my left hand.

I had barely put the first bite into my mouth when I saw the brigadier general nod to the lieutenant standing behind him, the same one who had commanded the detail that assisted at the mass grave site.

In a low voice, the brigadier asked the lieutenant in Arabic, 'Did you put some food aside for the old woman?'

The lieutenant said that he had.

Curiosity overcame me and I asked what they meant. The commander told me that about 10 kilometres away, within the area under the control of the Jordanian battalion, a Serb hamlet had been destroyed by a Croatian military unit. Its inhabitants had all fled except for woman in her mid-80s who refused to leave her home, or what was left of it, as it had basically collapsed from mortar shelling. The house did have a cement basement that somehow remained intact and held up the roof after the walls had fallen in.

The brigadier general said that after the old woman convinced her son, who did not want to leave her, to go away in hopes of finding safety elsewhere, the Jordanians had adopted the old woman and kept her son informed about his mother's condition. The Jordanians sent a Jeep with food for the woman every day, and whenever she complained of aches or pains, the Jordanian battalion doctor went and attended to her. This had been going on for months.

Again I was overwhelmed, this time by the Jordanians' kindness and by the reminder that human bonds endure in times of need, that dire conditions or situations can bring out the best – as well as the worst – in us.

This was true of my war experience, no matter where it was or who was involved, but the worst was much more prevalent. Perhaps this is why seeing the best was so extraordinary and heart-warming, recharging my human batteries after they had been depleted by the horrors of war.

The veneer of civilisation is indeed thin. Scratch the surface, and it disappears. But the Jordanians' kindness and other human gestures only increased my desire to pursue peace and justice.

I asked the battalion commander whether I could visit the old woman, and he agreed to let me accompany the lieutenant, the same one who had led the grave-digging unit, when he took her some food. When she heard the Jeep and other vehicles approach, the woman emerged from her basement through a passageway that the Jordanians had built for her and embraced the lieutenant and some of the men she recognised, hugging and kissing each one. She spoke in Serbian, and the men answered in Arabic. I could not hold back my tears of joy and gratitude to God.

The men gave her a plastic container with the *mansaf*, said something in Arabic that she did not understand, and pointed at me. She then came over to me, hugged and kissed me, and said things in Serbian that I did not understand. I hugged her and kissed her back. Even in this badly damaged house in a war-destroyed hamlet, hospitality was important to her, so we all followed her down into her basement, where she poured us tea (which the Jordanians had given her) in an assortment of glasses and cups. It was a happy gathering of people who understood each other very well because they spoke a common language, the language of the heart.

Back at the Jordanian battalion headquarters, I thanked the commander and promised to bring his unit's thoughtfulness to the attention of His Royal Highness King Hussein of Jordan, whom I knew well. After I did so several months later, King Hussein gave the brigadier general a medal and the battalion a commendation, and he had a Jordanian television station do a story on the battalion that included pictures that officers had taken of the grave site as well as the hamlet, the destroyed houses and the old woman. I later learned that before they were rotated out of the area, the Jordanians got the old woman out of her basement and secured transport for her out of Croatia and into Serbia, where her son was waiting.

December 1956: Cairo

IN THE 1950S, Cairo had trams, remnants of the 1930s and 1940s. Young boys commonly hopped on and off the trams, selling all sorts of goods: tissues, chewing gum or *semit* (the equivalent of pretzel bread covered with sesame seeds). These agile boys, whose ages ranged anywhere from 7 to 17, jumped from one rickety carriage to the other, hawking their goods to make a livelihood. The same was true on buses. One always worried that they would fall under a tram or bus, but that was their way of life.

The boys were only some of the estimated 20 per cent of Egypt's people who were officially unemployed and somehow managed to make a living, meagre as it might have been. Along with the tram sellers were young boys of the same age group who helped mechanics, electricians and carpenters in the Marouf area or shop-owners in the Boulak area. These barefoot, downtrodden, uneducated, poor kids also volunteered in Civil Defence units to help defend their country.

This manifestation of patriotism, the same patriotism that brought me back to Egypt from law school in France to fight for my country, came in the first three weeks of the war, between the end of November and the middle of December. While I, along with many others, was fighting or recovering from battle wounds, something unheard of happened in Egypt, something I suspect has never happened in any other country in the world: not one crime was reported in Egypt for almost three weeks, even though the streets had been abandoned by authorities. This total lack of governance was another result of the incompetence of the senior military commanders and the fact that the police had been called upon to take on a paramilitary function. What could have been a golden opportunity for burglars, car thieves and all sorts of other criminals turned out to be the exact opposite. It's possible that people simply didn't report wrongdoing or police didn't log crimes at the time, but in the cities of Cairo, Alexandria, Tanta, El Mansoura, Asyut, Suez and Beni Suef not a single crime was reported. (In the 1980s, I verified the absence of officially recorded crime by asking Egypt's minister of the interior, Zaky Badr, to have people to check the police reports for that time.)

Perhaps many criminals were just busy: although the minimum age to volunteer was 18, many boys as young as 16 found their way into Civil Defence units, surely including some who engaged in petty crime. As a training officer in the West Cairo district assigned to the army located in Marouf, I was proud of Egyptians from all backgrounds who came together in support of our nation.[6]

* * *

I was still very much acting on feelings of national pride and a wish to help my country as I made my way to my new assignment in December 1956 at Marouf camp, which was located at what used to be *Nadi Al-Shubban al-Muslemoun* (Club of Muslim youth), the equivalent of a Muslim YMCA. Its entrance was on a main artery in Cairo with a small building at the entrance that housed the command exercise field, about the size of an American football field. At the other end of the exercise fields were military reviewing stands, underneath which were some dressing and washroom facilities and storage rooms where we stored weaponry and ammunitions. A rotating group of ten soldiers and a sergeant were permanently stationed to guard the weaponry. A group of officers consisting of a lieutenant colonel as the commander, a major as his deputy, and a first lieutenant used the front area for an office. All three of the men were reserve officers, and one a senior unit leader of the National Guard who had the two gold stripes on his epaulettes. I held the rank of unit leader, with one gold stripe, though I was a training officer and thus not part of the command structure.

---

[6] Later, after my time in the National Guard was over, I discovered another extraordinary phenomenon. Sometime between the first week and last week of December, an estimated 1,000,000 Soviet semi-automatic rifles known as Caliber 7.62s were distributed to the volunteers in the Civil Defence units. The rifle was new to Egypt, as it had arrived only a few months earlier and was not widely used by the army. During my training in West Cairo, we were opening new crates and removing the grease from these weapons before distributing them to the volunteers for training use. The Soviet-made rifle cost 120–140 Egyptian pounds on the contraband market, and one could easily find a Soviet rifle in the Boulak district. In 1957, 150 Egyptian pounds was the average annual per capita income for an Egyptian, so for most of those who had volunteered in the Civil Defence units, one rifle was equivalent to a whole year's income. The head of military investigations, who handles information on stolen military goods, later informed me that fewer than 80,000 rifles out of 1,000,000 were not returned. Bearing in mind the composition of these units, I found this extraordinary. Not all the returned rifles could be credited to the honesty of the volunteers because many rifles were warehoused in the unit training camps, but the high number of returned rifles is a testament to people's loyalty to their country.

I had been so eager to get started that I hadn't realised that I simply had not been prepared by my training, which had been shortened from one year to three months to three weeks. Too much training, I feared, might mean that the war would be over by the time I was done, and all I had wanted was to graduate and get my stripe. I received my stripe but had no formal graduation ceremony or even a formal certificate of completion.

It all happened so fast that it left me with a feeling of uncertainty. I really did not know what was happening or going to happen, and coming from a background as privileged as mine, I did not like this sudden lack of control. Anyone with two or three stripes could tell me what to do, and I was utterly in the dark in terms of decision-making.

My duty assignment was from 0800 to 1600, during which I conducted training for the volunteers. Depending upon their training schedule, the volunteers, organised in units, came in at different times. I viewed this as a cushy assignment because I worked only eight to ten hours a day and could go home every afternoon and spend the night in my own bed. The camp was located in downtown Cairo, and my mother's driver often chauffeured me to the camp and picked me up at the end of my day. Social class definitely had its privileges.

While the job, for the most part, was unremarkable, one event stayed with me. One evening, almost everyone else went home for the night, but my position required me to stay overnight at the camp with a group of ten soldiers under my command. At about 10 o'clock in the evening, I heard a commotion in the street and asked the two guards posted there if they knew what was going on. The guards said that a crowd of people was running behind our camp to a spot where, rumour had it, an Israeli pilot had parachuted, presumably after his plane had been shot down not far away. I had been expressly ordered never to leave the camp while on duty, but I was sure that if the crowd reached the helpless pilot, they would kill him, so I ran back into the camp, gathered the remaining soldiers, picked up a machine gun from the arms rack, and rushed out the gate toward where I thought the pilot might be.

We soon learned that there was no Israeli pilot. Someone in a nearby building had hung laundry out to dry on a rooftop, a white bed sheet had blown off the roof, and somebody in the street had mistaken it for a parachute. I was relieved that there was no Israeli pilot in need of protection, but I quickly remembered that I had left my post without permission, which was a serious transgression.

Moreover, with so little experience in such situations, I made the mistake of documenting what had happened in the logbook, with nearly disastrous consequences: the next day my commanding officer said he wanted me court-martialled for leaving my post and the camp unguarded. I took a risk and pleaded my case.

I explained as best I could that part of my reasoning for disobeying orders was based on the Geneva Conventions and their requirements for how prisoners of war must be treated. Having completed my first year of law school at Dijon University, I was argumentative enough to convince him that if Egypt and its people were to be acknowledged as honourable enemies, no threat of harm should come to a prisoner of war. I then appealed to my commanding officer's moral compass and sense of honour. If his son had been shot down over Israel, I asked, would he not have wanted somebody in the Israeli army to save the son from an unruly crowd? What would others think of Egypt if an Israeli pilot fell behind an Egyptian camp and was slaughtered while the duty officer and soldiers in the nearby camp did nothing?

Something in my argument must have been convincing because as my commanding officer looked up at me from across his desk, a few drops of ink fell onto the logbook from the fountain pen he was holding. Whether he dropped the ink on purpose or I was just lucky I never knew, but the ink drop stained the page where I had documented the previous evening's events. The commander ordered me to rewrite the entry, and my rewrite did not indicate that the duty officer had left the camp without permission. I was spared a court martial.

Over the years, I thought of that experience every time I heard of a situation in which a prisoner of war was tortured or killed without those present doing anything to prevent it. It made what would otherwise be an abstract question very real. As history records, too many atrocities occur because so many of us are indifferent and uninvolved bystanders. Over time, I became convinced that if we can, we must act against wrongs no matter what the personal consequences may be. Our conscience, not regulations or social expectations, must dictate our actions.

December 1956–January 1957: Cairo

I CONTINUED MY work training volunteers, and my job went back to being just as boring as it had been before I thought I needed to save an Israeli prisoner of war. The drudgery was eased, however, after I was called to the front office to see the unit commander, who asked me to report to the regional command headquarters of West Cairo. The unit commander looked at me with curiosity, perhaps wondering why regional headquarters would call upon the lowest-ranking officer in his command.

I walked from the Marouf camp to Tahrir Square, about 20 minutes by foot. The offices of the West Cairo command were on Kasr el-Nil Street where it ended at Tahrir Square, which would later become famous on 25 January 2011, as the site of the demonstrations that ended the 30-year dictatorship of President Hosni Mubarak.[7]

Inside the regional headquarters on the second floor of a commercial building, a full colonel in the army reserve asked whether I spoke French fluently. I said yes, explaining that I had attended French Jesuit school from 1947 to 1955, that I had passed the French baccalaureate, and that I had attended law school in Dijon. Before continuing, the colonel told me that everything that followed was a military secret that I must not

---

[7] Mubarak was lieutenant general and chief of staff of Egypt before he became vice-president to President Anwar Sadat. Ironically, just as Nasser chose Sadat as his vice-president because he was the least threatening of the 'Free Officers', Sadat chose Mubarak as the least threatening among the senior military officers. Neither Sadat nor Mubarak was believed to be the brightest light in the chandelier, yet both surprised the world with their accomplishments and both, in the end, disappointed their people. No one in Egypt or elsewhere could have ever anticipated that Mubarak could be removed by a form of uprising after 30 years of dictatorship. But spontaneous popular demonstrations, completely peaceful, were able to bring down a well-entrenched dictatorial regime in a short period of time. The Supreme Council of the Armed Forces, under Field Marshal Hussein el-Tantawi, also played a decisive role in bringing down Mubarak, essentially because Mubarak had chosen his civilian Westernised and politically corrupt son Gamal to succeed him. Even though democracy did not survive the January 2011 events, the fact that this did happen was a truly exceptional event, not only in the history of Egypt but in the history of the world.

divulge to anyone. Would I volunteer to carry out a secret military mission? As far as I was concerned, anything was better than what I was doing, and I gladly agreed.

Then the chief of staff of West Cairo, an army captain, placed me in the hands of a master sergeant who ushered me to a chauffeured car and took me to the military area of Heliopolis. In 1954, the army had seized Heliopolis from the British, who had had military camps in that area of the city since World War I. (In another shameful example of taking public land and converting it to private use, this area, which covered several square kilometres, was used by the Egyptian armed forces while the military converted another area to housing for officers, who in turn sold their subsidised apartments and made good money on the sales.)

In one of these buildings I was taken from one office to another until I arrived in the presence of a major-general. In the strict rank-oriented world of the military, the equivalent of a second lieutenant is rarely summoned before a major-general, and this fact, along with my complete ignorance of what the meeting was about, filled me with trepidation. I immediately performed my best proper military salute and stood at attention until the major-general ordered me to stand at ease. The presence of more officers, who silently entered the room, made me even more nervous.

The major-general addressed me in a tone usually reserved for the admonishment of officers whose conduct has caught the disapproving eyes of those in command, but his words were not stern. He repeated the questions posed by the colonel at the West Cairo command. Did I speak French? How well? Why had I learned the language? And then a strange new one: did I know any Algerians?

I told him that I had known a number of Algerians from Dijon when I attended law school. Perhaps because of my nerves or the major-general's rank, I carried on with my answer, explaining that I knew some of them belonged to an anticolonial movement, which had many Algerians and other North Africans as well as sub-Saharan Africans, and that we frequently had political meetings and rallies and mounted demonstrations against French colonialism in North Africa and sub-Saharan Africa. He asked my impression of Algerians. What type of people were they? Were they really committed to fighting for the liberation of their country?

I answered positively, though I also made some critical observations about how rigid they were and how difficult they were to deal with. He nodded, as if agreeing with my assessment, and then said, 'Do you think you can train a group of Algerian volunteers who are going to Algeria to fight the French?'

The shrouds of mystery had finally been lifted. Perhaps because of my youthful presumption or manifest ego (which I was full of), I quickly replied, 'Yes, I can.'

The enlisted men spoke only French, he said. Could I handle that language well enough to teach them?

I again said yes, although in my mind's eye I recalled the difficulties I had had conversing with Algerians who had not received a high school or university education, whose French was mixed with colloquial Algerian, and whose accents I could not understand.

What about training men older than I was? Could I do that?

Again, I said yes.

Finally, he asked whether I could keep my work secret. Although I answered affirmatively, trying to sound as confident as possible, I had no real clue about what I was about to confront.

The major-general then stood in formal erect military fashion. After one of the officers in the room called everyone to attention, the major-general turned to me and said:

> You are hereby assigned an important national mission, and we are all depending upon you for its success. You will be training 220 Algerian volunteers coming from different parts of the world, mostly France, but many from Algeria. They risked their lives to come here, and they will go back to their country to risk their lives once again. You will be their trainer. Their lives and the success of their mission to liberate their country will depend on how well you train them. May God be with you.

What I did not understand then was that the 220 Algerians did not speak Arabic and that by the time the Egyptians had realised this, the Algerians had already arrived in Egypt. Telling these Algerians that their already-brief three-week training was to be postponed because the Egyptian military could not find a training officer would have been embarrassing – as would using a translator, especially a civilian one. I was in the right place at the right time, chosen to administer a basic training course only because I spoke fluent French.

* * *

I received more details from the major-general's chief of staff: I would be administering a basic training course for a period of three weeks at the Marouf camp, which would be closed to all other volunteers and trainings. The training had to be handled with the greatest confidentiality. To avoid attracting any attention, the trainees would arrive each morning in civilian clothing, and unless they needed nighttime training or drills, they would leave camp each evening in the same civilian garb. The programme would take only six to eight hours of active duty per day. Trainees were never to wear uniforms outside the camp; inside the camp, the Algerians would wear battle fatigues. If someone took a weapon out of the camp, this was to be reported up the chain of command on an urgent basis. No ammunition was to be distributed for purposes of live firing. For live firing, the Algerians would be transported to a military range under the supervision of another training officer. The list went on.

My superiors at the Marouf camp, I was told, had been told of my mission and would provide support. At 0800 the next day, I was to receive a sealed envelope from my commanding officer that would contain the names of the volunteers I would be training. I was ordered to keep the envelope in a safe location in the commanding officer's custody.

I knew that my new assignment had been fortuitous, based on language skills alone, but I was elated. I was no longer Second Lieutenant Bassiouni. I was Field Marshal Bassiouni. In my own mind, I was Napoleon. I went from being a guy at the bottom of the totem pole, waiting to see who would pick on him next, to being the man in charge. There would be supervisors at the camp, but since they did not speak French, I would basically be free to do what I thought I had to do. I was back on top.

The chauffeured car waiting to take me back to camp was a little more luxurious than the earlier one had been. By the time I arrived, my camp commander had left for the day, so I signed the roster showing that I had gone off-duty and returned home. I could not tell my mother about my latest assignment, and although I was excited, the more I thought about the task and responsibilities ahead, the more concerned I became.

* * *

My Algerian adventure began the next day. Just as I had been told, I received a sealed, official-looking envelope with the list of trainees. I saw at once that the volunteers ranged from 24 to 65 years in age, making every volunteer older than I was. I had little training compared to others in the military, but I knew that at least I had more training than these men.

The Algerians who arrived the following day appeared to be a motley crew. The men, all Front de libération nationale (FLN) members who had been involved in political work in Algeria and were now volunteering to fight on behalf of their country, ranged in physical appearance and strength as well as in age. Some were tall, well-built and physically fit, but these were the exception. Most were short and thin and appeared weak. I was most concerned about those aged between 45 and 65, as they looked old and physically unfit for military duty. Having just turned 19, I still considered anyone over 40 ancient, and I could picture these men as retired teachers or pharmacists – but certainly not military forces on the front line. I was soon pleasantly surprised, however, when these men, who turned out to be extremely tough, taught me how deceiving looks could be. They were determined, courageous and had nerves of steel, and in time, they proved both physically strong and highly moral. But I quickly learned that if I thought I could command them, I had another think coming. These men had their ways, and nobody was going to change that – no matter how hard I tried.

In this training, I had the assistance of only one man, a retired army major who served as my deputy. At the start, I asked him to put the men in line, dividing them into ten groups arranged in a U-shape for me to address. My initial instinct was to sort the men by their apparent fitness, but I decided that could be counterproductive, so I told my deputy to put at least three of the younger, fitter men in each group and spread the older ones throughout the groups.

As the men filed onto the training field, I cringed. With the exception of a few of the younger men, no one had a military bounce in his stride. That first day, putting the simple formation together took almost 20 minutes. Even the worst Egyptian volunteers I had trained in the Civil Defence services took only about five minutes to get into line, and that was bad enough.

As I came onto the field, my deputy issued an order in a booming voice: 'Attention!'

Watching the men, I didn't know whether to laugh or cry. They obviously had no idea what it meant to come to attention military style. (I later discovered that *not* preoccupying themselves with military formalities was a form of rebellion against authority. I had no doubt that these men were fiercely independent and extraordinarily proud and that they interpreted discipline imposed by any external authority as something as an affront to their personal dignity. But none of this helped me that day.)

As I began to address the men, I was quite nervous, but I did my best to appear calm and in command. I told them of my involvement as an activist at law school in Dijon, my participation in the anticolonial movement, and how I came to Egypt to volunteer for the armed forces to fight the colonial invasion of Egypt.

I was genuinely proud of my accomplishments (which to me seemed significant) and hoped that in hearing about them the Algerians might realise that we had common ground and that I shared their anticolonial sentiments, but these men seemed unmoved. (I now understand: in relative terms, I was a beginner in the struggle for human freedom and human dignity, and I still had much to learn in the way of sacrifice, pain and suffering. I grew up in an aristocratic and wealthy family, and I was just beginning to understand what it meant to fight for your freedom from people who looked down on you. While I had had some experience with racism when I was at law school in France, after I started my own military training and began working with the Algerians, I was forced to ask myself hard, uncomfortable questions. How could I feel the burden of racism when I had never felt discriminated against? Or poverty when I never wanted for anything? Or subjugation when I never bore it? I had so much to learn, especially before I could truly understand what so many of these men had endured for so long under colonial rule.) That day, in my ignorance I stood smugly at the centre of the formation waiting for my remarks to sink in and produce instant respect and admiration. After about five seconds, a man in the last row of the ninth unit raised a hand as if he were in a classroom.

"Monsieur l'officier", he said. His words were loaded with sarcasm.

I ordered the man to come front and forward and stand to the left of my deputy, the major. He ambled up and eventually reached us. I learned that he was 65, the eldest of the group, and a retired pharmacist.

Hoping to regain the authoritative upper hand, I addressed him as an officer does an enlisted man, ordering him to speak out loud and clear.

In a mild-mannered, soft but decisive voice, he thanked me for assuming the responsibility of the men's training but said he thought I should know that each unit would be commanded by someone appointed by the group's own leaders.

I struggled to keep my anger in check. How could an enlisted man challenge an officer, I thought. I was almost too shocked to speak. How could this man have the gall to suggest that a committee of men, not an officer, would choose a leader?

'Soldier', I yelled at the top of my lungs. 'This is an army! Not a parliament!'

He responded as calmly and quietly as before. 'Can we please meet in private to discuss this matter?', he asked.

My first instinct told me to order this man to clean latrines, but better judgement, perhaps born from my experiences with Algerians in France, prevailed. 'Bring your men and come to my office', I said in a low voice. My deputy told the other men to stand at ease, and I left.

In the office, before the delegation arrived I sat alone and thought about how best I could convey to them that under my command they would not have much room to manoeuvre.

None of the three men who finally showed up, all of them in their 60s, looked fit for anything remotely connected to military activity. Each man walked around the desk I was sitting at, introduced himself, and shook my hand.

At this stark violation of military protocol, I once again was torn between blowing up or taking it in stride. What other officer responsible for training incoming recruits, I wondered, would ever agree to sit with the recruits' elders and discuss command decisions, not to mention shake hands and use first names?

(I thought long and hard about this encounter later and realised that the elders probably behaved as they did because I was not an Algerian, not one of them, because I was young, and because I was in a position of authority that had absolutely nothing to do with their own community structure.)

That day, being challenged in my newfound authority by these trainees totally unhinged me. I almost went into a rage.

I was a very stubborn young man (and I think I am still now a very stubborn old man), but in the next instant I felt an absolute calm settle me, one I would attribute to divine grace. 'They aren't challenging your authority', I told myself. 'They can't reach you. It's their inability to reach you that is causing them to act in this way.'

I looked on these elders with a sense of paternalism. In retrospect, I know that this is not a conscientious way of treating others or achieving aims, but at the time I was too immature to understand that I had to be respectful of others, that I should attend to what others needed and felt, and that I was not above people simply because I had a stripe on my shoulder. I think that some embryonic awareness of the full equality of all people, even members of the military, was growing in me, but those feelings had not become an intellectual reasoning. It was as if some internal sympathy was constantly cautioning me, but I could not yet articulate it.

So, violating every form of military protocol I knew, I played host. I offered them tea. They accepted. After talking for 20 minutes, one of them said, "I think it is time we go back, and you can tell the men how we've decided to form the units."

We walked out of the office amiably, as a bunch of civilians would, with my extravagant military ego totally deflated. I was no longer a commander, but a consensus-builder. Unwise as this might have appeared, even to me, my instinct told me this was the right strategy. And I am grateful that I was wise enough not to resist.

Back with the other men, after my deputy called them to attention, I started with an apology. I said I was sorry to have kept them standing and invited them to sit on the ground, which they did with audible relief. I then described, as humorously as possible, what had happened in my meeting with the elders. They all laughed. The ice between us had been broken. We were on the same side. I knew I still needed to prove myself to these men, but I sensed they had accepted me.

I came to realise only much later that this first day of training the Algerians, when my instincts prevailed over my anger and frustration, were my first real lesson in leadership. I learned in that moment that leadership does not come from any insignia, rank or barked order. It is earned. Like so many other attributes or skills, leadership must be based on trust and conferred by one's fellows. After that first day of my hard lesson learned, the training mission went fairly well.

October 1993–January 1994: Geneva, Amsterdam and Chicago

THROUGHOUT THE CONFLICT in the territory that was once Yugoslavia, intense fighting and ethnic tensions affected everyone in the area, but as members of the UN Commission of Experts soon realised, sexual violence was particularly pervasive and especially damaging. This prompted commission member Fritz Kalshoven of the Netherlands to apply for a grant of $300,000 from his home country for an investigation into the systematic rape and sexual violence in the region.

But as October 1993, the one-year anniversary of the commission's establishment, approached, the funding had not materialised. While waiting for the money to come through, commission members recruited volunteers and designed methodology for a comprehensive study. But we soon hit another roadblock. According to UN rules, we were told, donors could not earmark contributions, so the Dutch government could not donate the $300,000 explicitly for the upcoming rape investigation. The UN then refused to accept the money from the Netherlands.

Outraged and deeply concerned that the stories we had heard could be lost in the conflict, I flew to the Netherlands and met with Pieter Kooijmans, the minister of foreign affairs, to find a way forward. Kooijmans was able to restructure the contribution without language restricting its use for the rape investigation, and I was able to assure him privately that the funds would indeed be used for that purpose, just as Dutch government officials had intended.

But still we were thwarted. Through the efforts of Ralph Zacklin, then deputy legal counsel to the UN Office of Legal Affairs (who I believe intended the Commission of Experts to have a modest record that could be easily discarded), the United Nations again declined the funding, this time citing an esoteric rule connected to accounting. Nevertheless, we plugged on with our work, and by December 1993 I was interviewing volunteers for the investigation.

As I became more involved in planning the investigation of how rape had been systematically used in the conflict, I began to understand the importance of not retraumatising victims with our work. Psychologists and psychiatrists were helpful, but they left me with a confusing abundance of information. So I reached out to women's and human rights organisations.

We held a meeting in Geneva with representatives from about 60 organizations. Half of the attendees represented women's organisations, and the rest were from human rights groups. The only man present, I opened the meeting by explaining what I hoped to accomplish through the investigation and what I hoped to gain from the meeting.

I had expected the response to be positive; it was anything but.

One speaker yelled that I was presumptuous to even *think* that I could conduct the investigation as I had described.

'You can't do it', the speaker said.

'Why?', I asked.

'Because you are a man', came the reply.

That sparked an argument between the women's organisations and the human rights organizations that went back and forth. I finally left the room, after asking those present to choose a leader, discuss my questions and tell me what to do.

A few hours later, three women from the meeting approached me and shared the group's conclusion. I should not conduct the rape investigation for a number of reasons, they said. I would retraumatise people. I would violate people's privacy. I would put their lives and family relationships at risk. Instead, they said, they should do the investigation.

I was stunned but undeterred. Still sure that with the proper guidance and support, I could conduct a thorough, respectful investigation, I convened a second meeting in the United States, in Detroit, where, I believed, people would want to contribute to such an undertaking. I gathered representatives from about 65 organisations, again making sure to include women's and human rights organisations, related my less-than-stellar experience in Geneva, and asked them what they thought of an investigation by the commission. To my shock, what happened in Geneva happened again: women's groups opposed the commission's conducting an investigation, and human rights organisations supported the idea. The opposition cited the same reasons I had heard in Geneva: the commission would mishandle the study. It would hurt victims all over again.

In the end, I took their concerns to heart. The number-one issue, I decided, was to avoid retraumatising anyone we spoke with. The second major concern was privacy. We needed to figure out how to protect the privacy of each individual we encountered and how to ensure that the data we gathered were not accessible to anyone outside the commission (including even family members). Those principles guided the design of our process.

As a next step, I consulted a number of senior psychiatrists in the United States. One of them, who had worked with American prisoners of war in the Vietnam era such as John McCain, provided me with much-needed guidance on how to speak with survivors of torture and other traumatic experiences such as rape and sexual assault. After talking with him, knowing that the vast majority of those we interviewed would be women and girls, I decided that these interviews would always be done by women. Some men did work on the investigation, but only women conducted the face-to-face conversations with victims.

December 1956–January 1957: Cairo

I F THERE WAS an overarching theme to my training of the Algerians, it was that my instincts were largely right – and yet I often had to learn my lessons the hard way. This was also true in my non-military life at the time, though one lesson there came from an unexpected but unsurprising source: my mother. As I was a 19-year-old man trying to make my own path in life, the maternal lesson, about the accommodations and acknowledgements that are the basis of respect for another person, involved a young woman. This was the very end of 1956, when the Egyptian monarchy was still in place. The Queen of Egypt, Queen Farida, was the head of the Egyptian Red Crescent, the equivalent of the Red Cross. She and my mother had been close friends since childhood: they had been classmates, Farida's father had served as guardian for my mother after her father died when she was young, and the two women had been bridesmaids at each other's weddings. When the queen assumed leadership of the Red Crescent, she insisted that my mother join the board.[8]

The building that housed the Red Crescent was adjacent to the camp where I was training the Algerians. Because my mother's board meetings often ended in the afternoon, about the time I went off-duty, one week we agreed to have a late lunch together downtown, taking advantage of her car and chauffeur. Shortly before our date, my mother mentioned that she would be bringing along a girl from the neighbourhood. This girl, who was 21, happened to be someone I had a crush on, and I was pretty sure the feeling was mutual. Until that point we had gone

---

[8] After the revolution, many of the aristocrats who were members of the board boycotted in protest over the appointment of Jehan Sadat, wife of Anwar Sadat, as the new president of the board. My mother was the only one who spoke out against the boycott and made efforts to reach out to Mrs Sadat. Because of this, she became the bridge between Mrs Sadat and the other women on the board, helping get their support when decisions needed to be made, and Mrs Sadat was always grateful to my mother for that. This was perhaps what got Mrs Sadat to introduce me to her husband later, which would lead to my having numerous personal audiences with him over the years.

out only in a group of young people, although occasionally during such outings she and I would hold hands. I was quite pleased to hear that she would be joining us for lunch.

At the camp where I was training the Algerians there was a Civil Defence unit assigned to guard that part of the city, and among the guards was an old classmate of mine, Guy, whose father was a doctor and who grew up two streets away from my childhood home. On the day I was meeting my mother and my crush for lunch after work, Guy was on guard duty. When a soldier is on guard duty, he stands in what is referred to as 'at ease' position, meaning the butt of his rifle rests on the ground while he grips the muzzle, with his arm is extended out at about a thirty-degree angle. His other hand is either at his side or behind his back.

As I was leaving camp that afternoon to meet my mother, I came across Guy as he was talking to a girl. To *my* girl. To my great aggravation, he appeared all too excited to be chatting with her. As the two were talking, Guy was holding his rifle with his right hand, and his left hand, instead of being behind his back, was holding a sandwich. Even with my own truncated three-week training, I could not believe Guy's conduct violation: a soldier on guard duty is supposed to stand at ease and refrain from speaking to anyone, and he is certainly not supposed to eat a sandwich. But Guy was doing just that, and he was doing it while talking to the girl I liked. In that moment, all my machismo came pouring out of me, and all the wisdom that I had marshalled with the Algerians left my mind.

'Who do you think you are?' I yelled at the poor fellow. 'You think you're a soldier? You're not behaving like a soldier!'

I berated him just as a drill sergeant does in the movies. Guy looked utterly humiliated as bystanders stopped to watch me chastise him. As I bellowed, I made sure the girl was watching. Guy immediately dropped his left arm, sandwich in hand, to his side. His mouth was agape in a mix of shock, horror and embarrassment, exposing a piece of partly chewed sandwich.

'Cherif! Stop it!'

Caught up in my self-importance and desire to humiliate Guy in front of my girl, I had not seen my mother approaching.

Her voice brought me crashing back to earth. I froze. In the centre of the crowd that I had attracted with my performance, in the presence of the soldier I had just humiliated (not to mention the girl), my mother proceeded to berate me in a way I had never experienced before – or have since.

'Who do you think you are? Just because some idiot put a stripe on your shoulder, do you think that makes you better than other people? How dare you embarrass that young man!' And on she went until she finished with, 'Get in the car!'

I quickly complied. Soldier or not, I knew this was not the time to anger my mother further. I got into the front seat of the car next to the driver, and my mother and the girl sat in the back seat. The driver headed straight home. Not a word was spoken all the way to the girl's house, and the silence was broken only by the requisite 'goodbye' she managed to utter as she stepped out of the car. When my mother and I arrived home, I went straight to my room and locked myself in. I was mortified by my behaviour. I had disappointed myself.

After stewing and reflecting a short while, I emerged and apologised to my mother.

'There is only one lesson I want you to take from today', my mother told me. 'You are not better than anybody else. Don't you ever think that because somebody put you in charge, you are better than another person. I thought I had taught you that.' She paused. 'When you speak to one of the servants, what have I taught you since you were a child?'

'When asking for something, always say, "Please"', I replied, feeling like a child.

'And then what?', she asked.

'And then when they do something for you, always say, "Thank you".'

'Does everybody do that?', she asked.

'No.'

'And that's the difference', she said. 'You really have to know that if you want the respect of others, you have to respect them first. When you ask with a "please" and you say "thank you", you're respecting the humanity of the other person, and they will respect you and your leadership. The same goes for when you are commanding men. Treat them with decency and respect, and they will obey you and respect you as well.'

That was one of the most important lessons my mother ever imparted to me, and I remember it as if it were yesterday. My early encounter with the Algerian trainees had made me trust my instincts, but this episode with my mother helped coalesce the principles of true leadership in my mind. I began to see that respect is a necessary condition of authority. The Algerian men were not challenging my command; they were asserting their dignity. I realised that if you want people to go fight and risk their lives for a cause, particularly when the order you have issued may lead to their death, you better at least give them the sense of dignity that conveys that you recognise that their lives have value.

After that episode with my mother, everything about the training programme seemed to fall into place. The trainees were not the most disciplined bunch, but their affection and respect for me and for one another were always clear and forthcoming. After our training for the day ended, a number of the men would come pat me on the shoulder and thank me, something you would never see a regular soldier do to an officer. The warmth and appreciation coming from the men buoyed me.

* * *

Two other incidents from my experiences with the Algerian trainees stayed with me. The first occurred during a night when I had decided to have the men stay overnight at the camp and serve as part of the night duty unit. On night duty, two Algerian trainees armed with rifles and bayonets were stationed at the front door, with two more at the camp's back door.

Despite the instructions from my superiors not to issue ammunition to the Algerians, I decided there was little risk in issuing ammo to the four soldiers who would be on night duty, along with the ten-man detail and the officer who would rotate on night duty. I had decided to stay overnight with the men in camp, and I stationed myself in a room under the reviewing stands, a raised platform from which the military leaders could observe what was going on in the field. At about 1 am, as I was resting on a small cot, I heard two shots fired in the air, the signal of distress. I jumped up from my cot, grabbed a weapon, and called for the men and sergeant in the nearby guardroom to follow me. The men accompanying me were all armed with weapons and ammo. We ran to the back-door entrance of the camp where the shots had been fired.

Both guards on duty, two of my Algerian trainees, had their rifles trained on about a half a dozen men lying face down in the dirty street with their hands on the backs of their heads. With only one bulb above the door, the street was dark, but there was enough light show that the men now on the street were all in Egyptian army uniforms.

When I demanded to know what had happened, the shorter of the two guards, Mohammad (whom I had nicknamed 'Little Mo') said, 'These men approached the door, and when we asked them for *kalimat el-sir* [the password], they claimed that they did not know it. One of them claimed that the man with him was a general coming to inspect the camp. As instructed, I fired two shots in the air to signify danger and ordered them to lie on the ground, facedown, with their hands over their heads.'

I saw that one man on the ground was indeed a major-general and another a full colonel. Little Mo's rifle was still trained on them.

Little Mo's rifle with bayonet was taller than he was, I remember thinking, and yet he had a major-general and five officers, including the commander of West Cairo, face down on the ground. I told Little Mo that it was okay let to let them into the camp, but he objected. 'No', he said. 'They have to say the password!'

I walked over to the major-general, who was still lying on the ground, and whispered the password to him. It was then that I discovered, to my horror, that he was the same man who had assigned me to the secret training mission. When I whispered the password to him with an accompanying apology, he paid no attention and repeated the word to Little Mo. Little Mo followed the proper procedure, saying '*Taqadam* [Come forward]', still holding his rifle trained on them. The other Algerian guard followed Little Mo's example.

As the major-general stood up, he turned to me and said, 'It is all right. You trained the men well.' He walked over to Little Mo and patted him on the shoulder, and Little Mo promptly returned to his position on guard duty, holding his feet slightly apart, with the rifle posed on the ground next to this right foot, leaning forward, in the 'at ease' position.

Although the major-general complimented me, the colonel was furious and ordered me to appear the next day, when he threatened to have me court-martialled for issuing bullets to the Algerians in violation of orders. However, he then begrudgingly said I would be forgiven for this transgression because the major-general had been impressed by the Algerians' training and discipline.

Many years later, I ran into one of the Algerian trainees and asked after Little Mo. Little Mo, the man told me, had died just a few months after that Cairo camp night duty, killed holding a position on a mountainside in Algeria. Apparently, he had been ordered to hold that position and keep any French from ascending the mountain. With only three men under his command, his troop was confronted by three French armored personnel carriers, each one with eight men and a machine gun on top. Little Mo held his ground as stubbornly as he had that night in Cairo. He and his three men died, the man said, and the French tossed their bodies aside. Such heroism is a true example of how the Algerians were able win their independence against an immense French force.

* * *

In the first weeks of January 1957, I was again struck by the integrity of the Algerian men who were willing to risk their lives to secure the freedom of their nation.

The authorities decided that the Civil Defence would be disbanded and set 24 January 1957, as the final date for all non-volunteer personnel to be reassigned or discharged. The announcement, which was read and posted at our Marouf camp, noted that a parade of all units in West Cairo before the commanding general for the city of Cairo would take place at a public garden at the tip of the Zamalek Island, linking Cairo to the suburb of Giza.[9]

A week before the parade, my Algerians, as I fondly referred to them, came in for a day-long training session. In a private meeting, the committee of elders asked me whether the Algerians were going to take part in the parade. After checking with my superiors, I told the Algerians what I had suspected: because of the intense secrecy surrounding their training, they would not be participating. The elders showed frustration and barely veiled anger.

Later in the day, when I went to the training grounds to see the men and my deputy called them to attention, no one moved. Every man remained 'at ease', even after the order to come to attention was repeated, this time in a louder, more authoritative voice.

What was going on? The group's leader responded from his place in the ranks: 'The Algerian contingent no longer wishes to receive training from the Egyptian military because apparently the Egyptian military does not deal with them with the dignity they feel is deserved.'

---

[9] The main bridge from Cairo to the southern part of the island is known as Kasr il Nil. At the other side of the island, almost exactly opposite Kasr il Nil, is the Giza Bridge, which leads to the mainland of Egypt and goes southward all the way up to the border with Sudan. This southern tip of the island is where the Presidential Guard headquarters and official headquarters of the Command Revolutionary Council used to be, sometime between August 1952 and 1956. The Presidential Guard continues to use the official headquarters, notwithstanding the various regime changes in Egypt. Opposite the bridge stood a big statue referred to as *Al Nahda* (the resurgence), intended to reflect Egypt's resurgence from being colonised by the Ottoman Empire and then occupied by the British to becoming a constitutional monarchy in 1923. That was when Egypt's first constitution was proclaimed, and when my grandfather, Mahmoud Bassiouni, became a member, and then president, of the Senate.

In 2014, in the middle of this square, Muslim Brotherhood and pro-democracy forces in Egypt clashed, and the military took over the country with a coup on 3 July. An estimated 200 people were injured. In this event and another at Raba el Adawiya square, an estimated 800–1,000 people were killed. I described both these tragic events in my *Chronicles of the Egyptian Revolution*, covering the period from 25 January 2011 to May 2014, when former Field-Marshal Abdel Fatah el-Sisi became president.

Today Cairo's opera building sits on the other side of Al Nahda square, but at the time, the land was the public ground where I received my initial training. It was also the site of the agricultural fairgrounds where at the 1926 formal dedication ceremony my grandfather broke rank to greet the son of his dear old friend.

The elders and I met again. Because they were prohibited from the parade, they said, they were ending their training and would have the political representative of the Front de libération nationale (FLN) in Egypt, Adda Ben Guettat, who supervised their presence in country, file a formal note of protest with the appropriate authorities. I could see the scene: Adda Ben Guettat, a broad-shouldered man who stood an impressive 6 foot 2 and always wore a *casquette*, a small cap with a visor, and square shaded reading glasses, would storm into the Ministry of Foreign Affairs (or worse, the Ministry of Defence) and raise hell about the offensive treatment of Algerian trainees by the West Cairo command.[10]

I believed that the Algerians were right to be upset about not participating in the parade, but I also understood the need for secrecy about their training in Egypt. I came up with a compromise plan that first needed the elders' approval: the Algerian group would march in the parade as part of the West Cairo unit, but its members would have to keep to themselves, not even talking or whispering to each other, so no one would know they were not Egyptians. The elders disliked having to keep their identities secret, which they thought showed that Egyptians wanted to conceal their support for the Algerians, but they agreed.

Then I needed to get the Egyptian military on board with the proposal. I went through the chain of command, though to the colonel commanding West Cairo, which I knew would be difficult because of the incident involving Little Mo and because the colonel had never liked the fact that despite my lowly rank I had complete authority over the Algerians' training. His reception was cold, and he kept me at attention while I presented my idea. He said only that he would pass the idea forward.

To my surprise, two days later my commanding officer informed me that orders had come from on high that the Algerians could participate in the parade. But he stressed the importance of total secrecy and total silence ... 'or else'.

Although his words were vague, I interpreted this to mean that if conditions were not met, I would be court-martialled and end up in prison. When I gathered the men in the courtyard and announced the decision, the men cheered and applauded, though the three elders, in private, later chastised me for not standing up for them sooner.

---

[10] Adda Ben Guettat was both a great patriot and true Algerian. In later years he became close to the FLN's commander during the war, Houari Boumédiène, who became the second president of the new free Algerian state and appointed Adda Ben Guettat as governor of Kabylia region.

On the day of the parade, I pondered what to do about weapons. The order for the men to march had not indicated whether they should be armed, and my inclination was to have them leave their weapons at the camp, since the general order for the training had prohibited any firearms outside the camp's boundaries.

But once again the Algerians took the lead. When I arrived at the camp grounds to prepare for moving out, the men were all holding their Soviet-made semi-automatic 7.62mm rifles with built-in bayonets. I looked at them with disbelief and helplessness, and I threw my hands open toward the sky, preparing emotionally for my court martial. The men, who saw my gesture as identifying with them as future liberators of their country, laughed and cheered for me. Truly, I thought, the Algerian sense of pride is enormous. Then again, so was mine.

My deputy, the major, put them in formation in lines of four. We were headed through the downtown streets of Cairo, and I made it a point to chart our course to go to Soliaman Pasha Square and from there to take Mahmoud Bassiouni Street to Midan al Tahrir. As we went down the street, I asked my deputy to pass the word to everyone to look up at the street sign honouring my paternal grandfather, the man who led Egypt's revolution in 1919 in Upper Egypt against British colonial rule. As I shared a piece of my family history with my men, I felt a new bond with the Algerians.[11]

When my Algerian men and I reached the parade grounds that day in 1957, we and other troops already gathered there were directed to sit by military police.

'You see', one of the elders said to me, 'They all have their rifles.' He was right: had I not let them carry their rifles, the Algerians would have been the only unarmed unit in the group, which of course would have made them look conspicuous. I stored this idea away in case I was later reprimanded, along with the sophistic argument that the parade ground, as a part of military facilities, was an extension of the training camp, where the men were permitted to carry weapons.

---

[11] At the end of the street, the northern extension of Tahrir square, an empty space was planted with grass and flowers; this later became the site for a statue of Lieutenant-General Abdel Moneim Riad, my second cousin and the chief of staff of the Egyptian Army, the man who had so passionately opposed my joining the military. That same intersection of Mahmoud Bassiouni Street and General Riad's statue, at the northern end of Tahrir square, became a symbol of the spirit of revolution for three historic weeks between 25 January and 11 February 2011, when the 30-year dictatorship of President Hosni Mubarak ended.

After an hour of waiting, we stood in formation, ready to file before the stands where the reviewing officers would soon be assembling. Two military police motorcycles came through the main gate followed by two jeeps full of MPs, as well as a full caravan of cars that we could not see because we were facing the opposite direction. The arriving officers then mounted the reviewing stands, and the Egyptian flag was hoisted at the centre of the parade grounds. A band played the Egyptian national anthem: *'Biladi, biladi, biladi. Lakihubbi wa fuadi. Mirs ya umm al-bilad ...'* ('My homeland, my homeland, my homeland. You have my love and my heart. Egypt! O mother of all lands ...'), and then the parade began.

The Algerians and I had been placed in the middle of all the units, probably to make us as inconspicuous as possible. Because the master of ceremonies was to announce every unit in the parade, I wondered how my unit would be announced; I assumed that secrecy would prevail and the Algerians would again feel deeply offended.

As we reached the centre of the reviewing stand, about three paces before the centre stage where the commanding general stood, I saluted, turned my head to the right toward my troops, and ordered, 'Right face!'

At this order, the 220 Algerians, all carrying their rifles on their shoulders, paused – and began to sing.

I can still hear their chorus, beginning with, *'Min Gibālina talac sawt el-ahrār, unadinā bil el-tiklāl ...'* ('From our mountains came the shouts of the free men, calling us to independence, calling us to independence, to the independence of our nation ...')

All 220 men were singing the revolutionary anthem, *Min Gibalina*, of their war of independence and continued in Algerian Arabic: 'Our sacrifice for the nation is more important than life. I sacrifice my life and my property for you. O, my nation, O, my nation, I love none better than you. My heart has forgotten the world and is lost in the love.'[12]

I thought to hell with the consequences and sang right along with them. I was sharing and rejoicing in their pride, perhaps as a mark of the bond we had formed during training. I felt that we had become a band of brothers, with the extraordinary solidarity that comes from knowing that your fellow soldier would take a bullet for you – and you for him.

We had barely passed the reviewing stand when a captain with two MPs demanded that we get off the parade grounds at once. I did so with

---

[12] Salah Sadaoui, *Min Gibalina (From Our Mountains)*, in *Qisat ala Hamza* [*The Story of Hamza*] (1950).

ominous dread, and we soon stood in the middle of the same empty round space where we had sat with the other units, which were arrayed all around the field but had been ordered to stop marching. As the senior officer descended from the reviewing stand and approached, I recognised him at once. He was the man who had initially ordered me to take over this training mission and the man Little Mo had held face down on the ground.

To my great relief and to everyone's surprise, the major-general, who was smiling, gave me a big hug, and said simply, 'I'm proud of you.'

A number of senior officers followed his lead and shook my hand, all of them apparently believing I was Algerian. After all, I had sung the revolutionary anthem with my men, in an Algerian accent no less. The major-general walked through our ranks until he saw Little Mo, patted him on the back, turned around to tell the other officers what Little Mo had done, and left.

Walking back to the camp, I again took Mahmoud Bassiouni Street, turning over what had just happened with my Algerians and the story of my grandfather on the same fairgrounds, leaving the king and his dignitaries to say hello to the son of Steta, who had delivered milk for his children every morning. There are times when you just have to do what you know is right.

There, on that day in downtown Cairo, the Egyptian Civil Defence was disbanded and my time in the military ended. While I was not the career army man I had dreamed of becoming in my youth, I had served my country, trained the Algerians to serve theirs, and – despite myself – gained some maturity.

As so often happens in my life, I have found circles back to that day and place. In April 2016, I received an electronic version of an article in *Al Masry Al Yom*, one of the largest daily publications in Egypt, with a story about Mahmoud Bassiouni Street in Cairo and M. Cherif Bassiouni Street in Chicago. I don't know how the journalist found out about the street in Chicago, but the article described these two quiet streets named after two men, separated by two generations, in two cities, so different and so apart. These little strings that tie past and present, through generations, across lands and oceans, remind me that our lives are inextricably connected, even when we don't expect them to be.

November and December 1993: Geneva

A FEW WEEKS after our fieldwork with the mass graves, I received a delegation of Serbian officials in my Geneva office on the fifth floor of the UN building overlooking the beautiful and placid Lake Leman. The head of the delegation was Zoran Stojanović, the Serbian minister of justice and a professor of criminal law at Novi Saad University, whom I had known from before the conflict, as I was the president of the L'Association Internationale de Droit Pénal (International Association of Penal Law) and he was a member of the Yugoslav national section.

Stojanović was accompanied by four men, one of whom stood out because he looked so menacing, full of restrained anger and perhaps hatred. His mere presence was jarring. He clearly resented the minister of justice addressing me with respect. In the minds of many Serb nationalists, I was a champion of the enemy, which consisted separately and jointly of the Catholic Croats and the Bosnian Muslims.

The minister had come to protest the fact that we had found only 19 bodies in the Poljana Pakračka area, where his government had reported to the commission that there were no fewer than 1,700 dead bodies. The implication was that the commission had been more diligent in searching for mass graves of Catholic Croats and Bosnian Muslims killed by Serbs than it was in looking for Serbs killed by the other two groups.

How could I possibly dispel the doubts of these men, I wondered. I told the truth. I explained to the men where we had looked, how we had conducted our search, the very difficult conditions we had encountered, and how we had found the 19 bodies. I then recounted the story of the Jordanians, the individual graves, the Serb Orthodox crosses, and our visit to the Serbian old woman. Fortunately, my military aide, Dutch Lieutenant-Colonel Anton Kempenaars, had taken pictures throughout our fieldwork, and he showed these to the men. He also showed photographs I had not realised he had taken: photos of the 19 bodies, including the woman in the white dress who was holding her shoes and hat so tightly against her chest.

The menacing man did not leave his chair and appeared quite skeptical of everything I said, but he must have caught a glimpse of the woman in the photograph that Kempenaars showed the other three men. He stood up very deliberately, his eyes bulging, and slowly made his way to the table, bending forward to where the photographs had been laid out. He took the photo in his hands, kissed it, pressed it against his heart and began sobbing. The man was about to collapse when two of his companions grabbed him and returned him to his chair, where he held the photograph to his heart and continued crying inconsolably.

The minister explained that this man was from Poljana Pakračka and that his entire family, including his fiancée, had been killed in the area. The woman in the photograph was his fiancée.

When I approached the man and expressed my sympathy, he looked up at me, stopped crying and said in perfect English, 'You found her, you buried her, and you treated her with dignity. For that I will always be grateful to you for so long as I live.' He then kissed my hand and asked if he could keep the photograph. I assured him he could.

The other men questioned me in detail about what I had told them, expressing both disbelief and admiration for how the Jordanian Muslims had buried the Orthodox Serbs with dignity and had made crosses to mark their graves, and how they had taken care of the old woman. Two hours later, with all of my scheduled appointments backed up, I had a hard time bidding them farewell. From that day, the vocal criticism of me from the Serbs subsided.

January–April 1957: Dijon

ON 28 JANUARY 1957, just four days after my military career in Egypt ended, I was back in France to meet with the dean of the University of Dijon to re-enrol in the law school. Luckily, despite the fact that classes for that academic year had already begun the previous October, the university accepted me, a decision that probably was the result of my standing before I left for the Egyptian military. Pleased to be back in a classroom, I threw myself into my studies with relish. I enjoyed my professors, my courses and my classmates. In no other time, before or after, have I studied with such pleasure and determination. I devoured every word I read, and it was as if a new world were opening. Yet there were challenges. My classmates were older than I was, and, as is to be expected of law students, very argumentative.

After the dean graciously welcomed me back to the school, I worked as hard as I could and within a month had caught up with three months of material. I loved the subjects, but I was also ravenous. We had civil law, criminal law, constitutional law (between first and second year), history of law, Roman law, and in the second year, a brand-new subject called econometrics. It is well established now, but at the time, reducing economics to metrics was a novel notion. Our curriculum covered the theories of John Maynard Keynes and the Austrian economist Joseph Schumpeter. The goal was to be able to make a legal decision as a government or private lawyer with an understanding of the quantitative dimensions, but from my perspective, it was a slog because we were obliged to take a course in political economy.

This was the time of many wars of independence in Africa, the anti-colonial movement and the war in Algeria, and the debates between students were heated. Despite my time in the military and in the working-class world of my French classmates, I was still seeing things from the perspective of the sheltered, elite family and society I had been raised in.

When I returned to Dijon, I was eager to see a Guinean classmate, Kemoko Keita, whom I had sat next to each day and who had helped me understand his upbringing, one vastly different from what I knew. Kemoko, the youngest of 12 children from a poor family, every day wore an old corduroy jacket that the nuns at his school had given him.

Other than the jacket, the only clothes he owned were two pairs of pants, two shirts and a sweater. His parents had put him in an orphanage because he was their 12th child and they could not afford to care for him. His father, a truck driver, was already struggling to make ends meet.

I could not imagine how Kemoko must have lived in his little tribe in Guinea, but he made many things come to life. We talked constantly, and he understood I was coming down from my aristocratic pedestal to where he and our other classmates lived. I was eager to learn, because for the first time I was really learning about others' lives, not only in sociopsychological terms but across the world, and specifically across Africa.

During these discussions, inside and outside the classroom, I never felt as if I were being bullied, pushed around or faulted for my lack of knowledge. Instead, with Kemoko's friendship, my eyes opened. Although at times our discussions could be critical, even intense, we never resorted to mean-spirited attacks.

In my first class after re-enrolling, I found that Kemoko had been saving the seat next to him even though he had no idea whether I would come back, and I gladly joined him on the high, uncomfortable wooden bench. Every day we walked together to the student restaurant for our meals and then went to a local café. There we would have a cup of coffee, and Kemoko would put a coin in the jukebox to hear the song 'Old Man River', his favourite. He did not understand English, but he was familiar with the French translations. Paul Robeson, singing in his deep voice about black workers along the Mississippi, was powerful. We listened to the song every day – Kemoko would put a coin in one day, and I would put one in the next. It was almost like a religious experience; we would sit in complete silence and lift that veil and carry on another day to go back and do the same thing. It was our form of meditation in place of prayer, a meditation on the human condition, before returning to our study hall or afternoon classes.

Kemoko and I did our work side by side. He had a winning smile and would always speak of me as the aristocrat or the rich boy, chiding me in a friendly way. I would laugh with him, but sometimes he would stop me and say, 'Do you realize what you just did?' And he would tell me his view of my actions, from the perspective of an African boy running on a dirt road without shoes.

I have much missed my friend Kemoko's counsel in the years since. In later years, I tried to track him down through appeals to non-governmental organisations and finally learned that he had become a judge in Kankan, Guinea, had been appointed 'Substitut Procureur Général' in Conakry, and that he had married and had one child. I learned that he had been arrested in 1971 and held in Boiro prison camp in a political and military purge that followed an attempted coup against President Ahmed Sékou Touré in 1970. I doubt that he survived.

Despite Kemoko's stewardship, however, I went on an ego trip. Soon after returning to France I went to the movies and saw a documentary reel on the success of France, England and Israel in defeating Egypt in the 1956 war. One scene I will never forget showed a huge pile of worn shoes. The Egyptian troops, the French commentator said, had fled the Israeli army after taking off their shoes because they preferred to run barefoot on the sand; the piles of shoes in the wake of their retreat was the proof. Then there was a picture of an Egyptian ship, the *Ibrahim*.

The *Ibrahim*, whose commanders I knew to be very daring, had undertaken a mission to bombard the port of Haifa, but after the bombarding its seamen had been forced to surrender. In the re-enactment of the *Ibrahim*'s surrender, the documentary depicted the Egyptian navy as cowards. This falsehood made me furious, and for days afterward I would stop those who had seen the movie. 'Listen', I said urgently. 'It was not this way. I was there myself.'

Perhaps my desperation came from the fact that so little had transpired since I had been in the Marouf camp, with one stripe on my shoulder, and since our brigade had lost 56 men in Port Said. Every night after that, I was in a different Algerian or Moroccan or Tunisian or African café, smoke-filled back rooms where everyone looked as if they were conspiring in the anticolonial movement.

I told stories of the war, and maybe I began to make some of them up. In my agitation, I talked about how the Algerians were going to beat the French and how fearless my Algerians had been. I got carried away with making speeches at meetings and to my peers, and the French secret police got wind of it. And, after a strange meeting at the Egyptian embassy in Paris regarding my student visa, the French police began to follow me.

* * *

A few days after returning to Dijon from Egypt, I arranged a meeting with the cultural attaché at the Egyptian embassy in Paris so that I could renew my student visa and have my small student stipend reissued. The meeting was supposed to be routine. I just needed to meet with the man in charge of handling the affairs of Egyptian students in France, one of the few employees left at the embassy after the 1956 Suez War.

I arrived at the embassy anticipating a brief, pro forma meeting, but as soon as the meeting began, the man charged with handling student affairs asked me about my training of the Algerian unit and said he had seen newspaper coverage of my receiving the medal of merit for fighting in the Suez. Did I know the director of the Egyptian intelligence agency, this man asked. I said I did. But then the meeting turned downright bizarre when my questioner looked me straight in the eye and asked, 'Do you have the code for the safe?'

I told him that I did not, and although I could tell he doubted my answer, I soon extracted myself from his office. Only later did I learn that my questioner and his wife were double agents; in retrospect, I think he must have believed I was just being coy, although of course that was not the case. Unbeknown to me, the French secret police began to follow me after that meeting. They followed me until 23 April, when my life turned upside down.

After not receiving my new student visa for weeks and then months, I figured there must be some mistake and went back to the embassy to retrieve it. When I arrived, however, the embassy officials refused to give me my application. Not knowing how best to proceed, I consulted an official at Dijon University, who told me to seek out a professor of administrative law, who investigated on my behalf and found that my application's status was normal. On this basis, the dean announced my problem at a faculty meeting and, in a touching move of solidarity, the entire faculty signed up as my attorneys, with the administrative law professor as the lead attorney. They all signed a petition to the French administrative courts to renew my visa and allow me to continue my studies uninterrupted.

* * *

A few days later, on 23 April, I stepped out of my door at 8 am and found three men waiting on the landing. They looked unmistakably arrogant, like police. They surrounded me and said, 'Mahmoud Bassiouni', mispronouncing my first name and Italianising my last. I responded firmly and calmly in the affirmative, but a chill ran down my neck. I kept myself under some control, but, even now, I can still feel the intimidation of that confrontation and what followed – the fear that set in a few hours later and then, over two days, turned to terror.

The senior officer ordered me to accompany the men to the prefecture to answer questions about my visa extension request. Somehow, that reassured me, since I knew I had done nothing wrong, although I had thought the normal procedure was to send a 'Notice to Appear' at what was effectively the immigration division of police headquarters. A black Citroën was waiting, engine running, with an officer in the driver's seat. As I stepped through the front door, the officers told me, 'You're under arrest for subversion.'

'Why?' I blurted out. I spoke excellent French and was a bright kid; I knew enough about the law and was well accustomed to being argumentative. I began to argue, but they told me to shut up, and I was bundled off to their offices. From there I was transferred to the offices of the prefecture. I kept arguing with them, confined in the back seat, hoping one of my points would make them think twice.

'I'm using the constitutional rights of anybody to speak. I'm speaking openly and publicly – I went to cafes. Where else do you want me to go?', I asked.

I wanted to them to understand that I was a naïve kid who was studying law and believed that I had a right to speak.

'What subversion?', I said. 'I'm speaking publicly! The government is making a mistake! I'll make the same speech here.'

I do not think they could recognise the principled position I was coming from. Maybe it was so bewildering to them that in the final analysis it was to their benefit. I was not ominous or frightening or threatening, and I did not have the appearance or demeanor of somebody violent. I was just somebody full of naiveté, enthusiasm and idealism, the sense of justice and fairness that is very much a part of youth. I was a young person – one not yet tarnished by *realpolitik*.

* * *

I was seated in the back of the car between two officers, and the apparent leader sat in the front. It was a short, ten-minute drive. My mind was racing in all directions, not knowing what to focus on, even as I was talking. How did they know that I usually left my room for classes at about 8 am, I wondered? It hit me that I must have been under surveillance. But, for what? I did not venture much further than from school to the student cafeteria for meals, a popular café at the city's main circle back to school, dinner and home. I had copious studying to catch up with, and spent every possible hour on it. Why, then, would the police follow me? How could it actually be for the visa renewal application?

Gradually the suspicion overtook me. Could this calamity be the fault of the crazy operative in Paris, the man charged with student affairs in Paris who had been convinced that I was an Egyptian secret agent? I turned over the possibilities. It must have been his doing. He had seemed so peculiar, almost paranoid. Then again, I thought, he was an Egyptian official and would never betray his country – and yet, why not? On went my whirring, until we reached the prefecture. In a third-floor office in the back of the building, still accompanied by the same three officers, fear started creeping in. I was seated at a table facing what appeared to be a one-way glass window, as in the movies, and I was left for about ten minutes to stew in my juices. The technique is the same everywhere, but it worked on me because I was in panic, accused of doing something wrong and in need of defending myself, but I did not know what had made me a target. I've since concluded that I worked myself into a state of denial in that little room, putting aside dread and reality. Certainly, I did not dare then think of what was publicly known of the rampant torture employed by French security against suspected members of the Front de libération nationale (FLN) and its supporters.

Two burly men came in. One sat opposite me; the other stood behind. The interrogation that followed was similar to those in movies. At first, a few routine questions: name, parents' names, date and place of birth, address in Dijon, other addresses, addresses in Egypt, parents' occupations. And then came the probing: was I a member of the FLN? An affiliate, a supporter? Did I work with them? Did I know anyone who was an FLN member? Then the most critical questions: was I an officer in the Egyptian army? Did I train FLN Algerians? Was I sent to France to continue to work for the FLN? What was my mission? Who were my contacts?

I answered all the questions truthfully and with self-assuredness because I did not feel I had anything to hide. Yes, I served in the Egyptian army, which was not a crime, even in France. Yes, I trained Algerians under order from my superiors, and that was not a crime in Egypt. But then came the retort from the imposing man in front of me: that was a crime in France, and I was on French soil now. At this juncture I could no longer deny to myself that I was at the mercy of French security apparatus, the Département de la Sûreté Territoriale, and likely to be tortured.

That moment was one of the most fearful of my life, and my fear must have been visible. The interrogators asked if I would cooperate, offering the usual leniency one also sees in the movies – and I agreed because I knew I had not done anything wrong.

They asked for a narrative, and I am fairly sure that I said what I have recalled here, though I did not think they needed to be told of my strong identification with the Algerians. I omitted the episode about the military parade and the singing of '*Min Gibalina*'. The sticking point for my interrogators was the identity of the 220 Algerians. I kept telling them that I knew only their first names, and I was not even sure whether those names were real. I sensed they would be pushing that point harder. Somehow, I must have come across frightened and truthful enough to warrant a reprieve.

They left me alone in the room for about two hours, after what I think was about two hours of questioning. They had taken my watch, and the room had no window. I was exhausted, worn out, hungry, thirsty and tired. There was no food or water. An intense bright light shone on my face, and I was too afraid even to move.

I waited. The delay seemed interminable. I could not think at all. It was as if I were in a deep, dark well, even though strong light was bearing down on me. Above all, I felt alone. No one knew where I was, no one could rescue me. I was at the mercy of people who I knew had no mercy. To them I was the enemy, one who had trained others to kill their own.

All that mattered in this interrogation room was whatever the secret police wanted to attribute to me. And what they imagined I knew – but concealed. From this premise, to extract information from me by any means would be to save one or more of their own. If nothing else, I could not evade punishment for supporting their enemy. There was no question in their minds that they were right, and no doubt that I deserved whatever was coming to me. But what could I do? Nothing – I had no information to give, even if I wanted to, and under torture I probably would have said whatever they wanted, implicating or accusing people I did not even know. This is how torture functions. And yet security services continue to rely on it.

Little did I know that the psychological torture would soon end, but that a few months later it would start all over again, this time at the hands of my compatriots. And little did I know that there, by the grace of God, I escaped physical torture and that many years later I would co-chair the Committee of Experts that drafted the UN Convention against Torture.

Yet in the dragging afternoon and evening of 23 April 1957, I was in another world. By what I assumed must have been 8 pm, 12 hours after I had been removed from my lodging in Dijon, I was given a sandwich and a small plastic bottle of water. I ate and drank, put my head on the table, and fell asleep.

Early the next morning I was awakened, handcuffed and taken downstairs and out of the building through a rear door to a courtyard where the same car waited for me, at the same time of day as it had the day before. The security officials drove almost five hours to a drab grey-stone building that I did not recognise. I could see little of the terrain, as the back windows of the car had black curtains.

I later found out I had been transported to a security facility adjoining the Paris courthouse. We passed through a steel gate that ominously clanked behind us. I was taken down to a cell and my handcuffs were removed. I wasn't interrogated until what I assumed was almost midnight, the end of 24 April and the start of 25 April, when I was taken to an interrogation room. I had been awake for 17 hours that day and probably 20 hours the day before.

The line of questioning was unchanged from what I had endured the day before and went on until I collapsed, possibly near 2 am on 25 April. I do not recall much other than being taken back to my cell, but no one had laid a hand on me yet. I was truly unsettled. I was not yet 20 years old, the son of an aristocratic family, with nothing to prepare me for any such encounter. I was attuned only to survival, and without hope. During the daylight hours of 25 April nothing much happened. I was left in the cell all by myself, received three relatively decent prison meals, and was totally out of sorts – but grateful for the respite.

I had been in custody in Paris for about three days. I was questioned and repeated the same answers, but by the third interrogation I was much less fervently insistent and much more afraid. The knowledge that the French tortured and killed people in this prison never left me. As time passes in isolation, a kind of seizure sets in: you don't know where you are, you don't have any idea whether anyone knows or cares where you are, and you have no way to find out.

My youthful naïveté could not have been very impressive when I talked about the war days in Egypt. Held without cause or recourse, however, it turned out to be one of my saving graces. What I said under the pressure of my interrogators was the truth and would have been far too artless, not to say stupid, to have been the guise of an undercover agent. In addition, the dean of the Dijon Law School, Jean Portemer, to his eternal credit, sent a letter of protest to the prefecture as soon as he had word of my arrest, and delegated the professor of administrative law to represent me again. He, too, sent a formal letter to the prefecture and filed a petition before the administrative court to request my immediate release. Never before had the faculty taken such initiative for a student. The pivotal force, as has been the case time and again in my life, was my grandfather and his friendship with Mahatma Gandhi.

1930s: Cairo and Various Ports and Cities in India

OF ALL MY grandfather's exemplary qualities and actions that have served as touchstones, it was his pacifism that ultimately secured my release. When my grandfather led Egypt's 1919 revolution against the British in Upper Egypt, he never engaged in an act of violence, and he led popular demonstrators with a white umbrella, undaunted even in peril when the British forces opened fire on the crowds. In early 1936, years after facing a death sentence and imprisonment in the desert and rising to become president of the Senate, my grandfather was reading the weekly magazine of his party, the Wafd party, called *Al Mussawar*, which was Egypt's equivalent of *Life* or *Time* magazine, edited by an old friend named Mahmoud Aboul-Fath. He came upon a story about a man called Gandhi who was leading Indians in their struggle for independence from the British by mounting a non-violent campaign. The Mahatma, as the Indians reverently called him, was photographed draped in white woven cloth that resembled what Muslims wear on their annual *hajj* pilgrimage to Mecca. But the image that caught my grandfather's eye was of Gandhi leading a massive demonstration with a white umbrella. Mahmoud Bassiouni was so taken by this figure that he asked Aboul-Fath to lunch so that he could hear more about Gandhi. Aboul-Fath regaled him with stories of the Indian lawyer, who early on worked in South Africa and was a populist leader. My grandfather, captivated, asked Aboul-Fath to arrange for him to go to India to meet this extraordinary man. He wanted to express the support of the Egyptian people, who only thirteen years earlier had won their formal (though not de facto) independence.

Aboul-Fath somehow succeeded, and in late 1936 my grandfather, along with Aboul-Fath and two others, went by ship from the Suez to Bombay. In the photographs, my grandfather wears a dark-red felted Egyptian fez, which must have looked strange to the Indians he encountered. The real problem for this mission of solidarity was language: my grandfather spoke only Arabic, while Gandhi did not. Any communication was conducted through Aboul-Fath, who spoke English.

When our family's cook, Usta Mohammad Mustafa, first told me this story, when I was around seven years old, it seemed funny to me that these four wise and distinguished men with fezzes on their heads travelled to India to seek out a man they did not know, in a place they did not know, who spoke languages that only one of them could understand. The expedition might as well have been the stuff of epics and fairy tales. But these four Egyptians did land in Bombay and began enquiring where they could find Mr Gandhi. When asked who they were, they enthusiastically responded that they had come on behalf of the Egyptian people to give moral support to India's independence movement. Their declarations earned them warm greetings from almost everyone they encountered, and soon, after several trains and several days, they were escorted by kindly volunteers to see Gandhi.

My grandfather told me that he first saw Gandhi sitting on the floor, using a hand-operated loom to make cloth out of cotton. He said he was so thin that he almost looked haggard. His head was shaven, and he wore white metal-framed glasses that did not seem to fit. The first encounter was clumsy: the Egyptians expected Gandhi to get up and greet them, while Gandhi expected them to get down on the floor next to him and put their hands together as in prayer, a gesture of peace. The cultural divide soon subsided as Gandhi, smiling, listened to Aboul-Fath transmit my grandfather's fervent sentiments. And when Aboul-Fath told him about my grandfather leading demonstrations with a white umbrella, he erupted in laughter and then lifted my grandfather's fez and kissed him on the head. The whole assembly broke into cheering and laughter, including Gandhi's aide, a young Jawaharlal Nehru, who became India's prime minister after independence in 1947. When my father, Ibrahim, was posted as Egypt's deputy chief of mission to India in 1949 and later in 1951 as acting ambassador, Nehru fondly remembered the gesture of Mahmoud Bassiouni, who travelled for weeks from Egypt to see Gandhi and express solidarity with the Indian people. For Nehru, in turn, my father was a favourite among foreign ambassadors, and Nehru always made him feel warmly welcomed in India. My release from arrest in France was born from their friendship.

April 1957: Paris

A S I WAS sequestered in a holding cell in Paris, Egypt's Minister of Foreign Affairs Mahmoud Fawzi received word of my detention through the last diplomatic dispatch from the man in charge of handling the affairs of Egyptian students in France on 23 April, the day I was arrested and the day the man and his wife resigned and went underground. The news of my arrest and the discovery of the double agent who turned me in reached the director of the Egyptian General Intelligence Agency (GIA). Betrayal is not something any intelligence body takes lightly – it is the ultimate crime for a security apparatus – and I went up in the GIA's estimation for having smoked out the double agent, even inadvertently. The director apparently let the foreign minister know that every effort should be made to get me out. What followed was another twist of fate.

Minister Mahmoud Fawzi called my father and told him about my imprisonment in France. When my father asked what could be done, the minister answered, 'Nothing. We don't have diplomatic relations with France anymore.' Yet Fawzi suggested that my father, as former Egyptian ambassador to India, call Prime Minister Nehru for help. My father telephoned Nehru, calling upon the connection he had with my grandfather and on their own friendship. My father shared with him the little information he had, saying that I had been arrested in France because I had trained Algerians in Egypt in 1956. Luckily, Nehru was responsive – at the time, he was one of the primary leaders of the Non-Aligned Movement (NAM), along with Egypt's Nasser, Yugoslavia's Tito, and Sri Lanka's Sirimavo Bandaranaike. The NAM had been established at an international gathering in India in 1955 to stand up to colonial powers – so to support Egypt and a struggling Algeria was not something Nehru could walk away from.

Again to my good fortune, Nehru was a good friend of UN Secretary-General Dag Hammarskjöld, who was also sympathetic to the NAM and committed to peace and human rights. Hammarskjöld, in turn, called the French minister of foreign affairs, Christian Pineau, telling him that this request was an informal *démarche*, a euphemistic diplomatic term to describe an initiative 'not for attribution.' The exceptional nature of the UN secretary-general calling one foreign minister on behalf of another important country's prime minister, who was himself acting on behalf of Egypt, which had been the centre of the world's attention only months earlier in the 1956 war, can hardly be overestimated. Pineau, quick to react to the *démarche*, called the French minister of the interior to inquire about the arrest of an Egyptian student named Mahmoud Cherif Bassiouni.

France had already suffered embarrassment at the Security Council a few months earlier when it had been ordered to withdraw its troops from Egypt, and it was also in the midst of a bloody campaign in Algeria that went against international public opinion. As common-sense governmental practice, the minister's staff inquired and found out about this student in Dijon who had been turned in by a double agent as a possible high-powered Egyptian intelligence operative. The only problem was that the almost-20-year-old young man did not fit the profile of subversive actor: I attended class every day and had a reputation as a serious and hard-working student with no bad habits. I was active in the anticolonialist movement, but that was the extent of my threat. In light of these facts, the minister of the interior asked for a thorough review of my file.

After my midnight interrogation and a full day of sitting in my cell, the next day, 26 April, I was awakened at 6 am with breakfast, taken to a bathroom, given a bar of soap and a towel, and asked to take a shower and wash my hair, which I gladly did. I was then taken to an office, where I waited with mounting hope – hope that I had been found by my father or someone who was using any leverage or influence available to get me out of this predicament. I hoped that the tide might be turning, but I did not know how. Around 10 am I was taken out to the same courtyard where I had arrived days before to another waiting car with another team of four police officers, and we drove out the steel gate and out of Paris. Without a word of explanation, I was taken in an unmarked Peugeot on an eight-hour drive to the Swiss border near Geneva.

* * *

At the border, the officer sitting in the passenger seat got out of the car to meet two uniformed Swiss police officers and two other men in civilian clothes. I was still sitting uncomfortably in the back seat with guards at each side. Then came the signal by the French team leader, and I was let out of the car. The team leader gave my passport to one of the uniformed Swiss police, and salutes were exchanged. The French went back in the Peugeot, made a U-turn, and returned in the direction of Paris. My arrest in Dijon, transfer to Paris and then removal to Switzerland had all been accomplished without a paper trail, except for the denial of my request to renew my student visa, which was at the discretion of the granting authority. The Département de la Sûreté Territoriale had covered its tracks.

One of the men in civilian clothing approached me, saying in Arabic, '*Al-hamdella bissalama*', 'welcome in good health', and he gave me a strong handshake and then a hug. His name, as I would soon learn, was Wahid Ramadan, Egypt's military attaché to Switzerland, and he had come all the way from Bern to receive me. Wahid Ramadan had been in the second tier of the Free Officers responsible for Nasser's revolution in Egypt in 1952.

Wahid Ramadan was tasked with picking me up, and the first place we stopped was a café. I had coffee and a croissant, and he said he had booked a room for me in a small place in Geneva. When we reached the city, Ramadan offered to send an assistant with me to help me buy clothes and invited me to dinner later that night, which I accepted. At the dinner, when he asked me what had happened, I recounted all that had transpired since 23 April, and he was able to shed light on some circumstances. According to Ramadan, the Egyptian military attaché in Paris, a man named Sarwat Okasha, left the Egyptian embassy when the two countries ended their foreign relations, before I had returned to Dijon. Before he and the rest of the diplomatic staff departed, save for a few, including the man who had been responsible for students, Okasha had a budget from Egypt to fund leaders of the Algerian liberation movement in France, a scheme that the French intelligence had learned of. Okasha had guarded the information about whom he funded to support the Algerian revolution in files in his safe in the embassy, but he burned the majority of those incriminating documents before he left for Egypt. Okasha did not burn all the files, however, and those documents that he had spared remained stored in his safe. He had told the man responsible for students that someone would eventually come with the combination to the safe and retrieve the files. The man responsible for students, who stayed on in France, was tasked with taking that person to the safe.

Suddenly, the strange questions the man had asked me when I was applying for the renewal of my student visa began to make sense. What Okasha did not know at the time he left France was that this man, who was married to a French woman involved in French military intelligence, was acting as a double agent for French intelligence services. He had secured a job for his wife as the Egyptian ambassador's secretary, perhaps to act as a plant. I suspect that after my meeting, the operative must have thought I was the person Okasha sent for the files but that I was being coy.

Distrustful, as a double agent would be, the operative probably had French intelligence follow me. Then, when the French heard me spouting anticolonial views and support for the Algeria revolution throughout cafés in Dijon and learned that I had trained Algerians to fight against France, I was labelled an agitator, someone who had to be arrested for subversion.

Although I did not know this at the time, Ramadan and Okasha were both in the GIA and hated each other. After hearing my side of the story, Ramadan took the opportunity to get back at Okasha, and after our talk sent a report to the director of GIA, basically saying that I had been arrested because Okasha was an idiot, that Okasha did not realise that the operative was a double agent and kept him around, and that all the Egyptian secrets were now known to French intelligence. He cited our conversation.

Okasha, who was back at the GIA, got the report and was clearly angry at Ramadan – and because Ramadan said that I had told him everything, he was angry with me, too. I made an enemy of this man without even knowing it.[13]

---

[13] Prior to all of this, Wahid Ramadan had established something called Kataib al-Shabab (Youth Brigades), which was a paramilitary force. It was dissolved by the government in 1957 because Salah Nasr, director of the GIA, believed that Ramadan was preparing a military coup against Nasser. Ramadan was then placed in Switzerland. Upon my return to Egypt, I learned that Ramadan returned to Egypt after his report, presumably to confront Sarwat Okasha about the French embassy. But he was arrested, kept in prison for more than nine months, and was so badly tortured that his legs became paralysed. After a long period of recovery, he could walk with two canes, but he was still kept under house arrest – all for making that report. He died shunned by his peers.

April–June 1957: Geneva

D ESPITE THE EVENTS that took me there, I had an exciting time in Switzerland. Knowing I would not be welcome in France, at least in the near future, after arriving in Geneva I called the dean in Dijon, and he contacted the dean at the University of Geneva. The law school dean in Geneva, Jean Graven, was gracious and kind and told me that the faculty in Dijon was petitioning to have me come back for a week in June to take my final exams. I had not forgotten that this was my last opportunity to complete law school in France in three years, and my sense of urgency was unabated.

Everybody was convinced that I would get the visa to take my exams and then return to Geneva, so the dean of Geneva's university registered me in the graduate programme for international law as a substitute for my courses in Dijon. The only class I took my first quarter was a seminar taught by Paul Guggenheim, who at the time was probably the most famous European professor of international law. Guggenheim, a German Jew who had immigrated to Switzerland in 1932, had been a professor at the University of Zurich before moving to Geneva.

What I did not know at the time was that Guggenheim had been the legal advisor to the Conference of the Suez Canal Users' Association, as it was called in 1956. To show their concern about Egypt's ability to administer the Suez Canal, the British and the French had called a conference in London and invited all the countries that used the canal. As a way for Britain and France to justify their use of force to control the Suez Canal, British and French officials argued that Egypt was not able to guarantee freedom of passage through the canal, which was required under the 1888 Constantinople Convention that Egypt had signed. If they could prove that Egypt was not able to provide this freedom of passage, Guggenheim argued, their continued jurisdiction over the canal was justified.[14]

---

[14] I did not know this at the time, but Guggenheim was also the legal advisor for the Jewish Agency, the principal organization that funded the immigration of Jews back into Palestine and their settlement there. The agency was mostly funded by the Rothschilds in France. Coincidentally, the loans the Egyptian government took to help build the Suez Canal were funded by the Rothschilds in Britain and France, and it was when they were afraid they weren't going to get their money back that they convinced the British to attack and occupy Egypt in 1883, which in some ways was a parallel to the events of 1956.

Guggenheim was a short fellow, rather heavy-set, and wore a three-piece suit with a watch and gold chain. He looked like Hollywood's image of the quintessential law professor from Harvard in the 1900s; he was very arrogant, perhaps rightly so. There were about 14 or 15 students in the seminar, all older than I was, but somehow Guggenheim had heard of me. The first day he looked at me and said in French, 'You're the Egyptian. I understand you fought with the Egyptian army.'

'Yes', I replied. 'I had the honour to do so.'

He looked at me sternly and said, 'You will write your paper on the illegality of the nationalisation of the Suez Canal.'

I told him that with all due respect, I would like to write on the legality of the nationalisation of the Suez Canal.

'Well'. he said, 'If you write on its illegality, you will qualify. If you write on the legality, I think you've already flunked.'

When I told him, in front of the class, that I would let him be the judge, he seemed flabbergasted.

Dean Graven later called me into his office and said, 'I hear you had problems with Professor Guggenheim.'

I told him I had not had any problems, but he pressed on. Did I know that Guggenheim had been the legal advisor to the Lancaster House Conference, the meeting of the Suez Canal Users' Group? And that he had been the main architect of the legal argument for the invasion, which was that the nationalisation of the canal had been illegal? 'And now', the dean said, 'you're going to write a piece on the legality of it?'

I was undeterred.

As Dean Graven and I talked, I learned two things that would become central to my future. He was president of the L'Association Internationale de Droit Penal (AIDP – the International Association of Penal Law), which had been founded in Vienna in 1889 and reorganised in Paris in 1924, and introduced me to that organisation's work. (How was I to know then that I would later become the association's secretary-general and then its president?) I also learned that he and his son, Robert Graven, had been commissioned by the emperor of Ethiopia, Emperor Haile Selassie I, to write a model penal code for Ethiopia. In this model penal code, Dean Graven introduced three provisions that were exceptional for legal conventions at the time: one against genocide, one against crimes against humanity, and one against war crimes. He was setting up a team of six students to help draft these three provisions, and I accepted his invitation to participate, which led to my contributing to the drafting of these provisions in the Ethiopian criminal code in 1957. Many years later, I had the opportunity to participate in a similar drafting process for the International Criminal Tribunal for the Former Yugoslavia and the International Criminal Court (ICC).

In yet another example of how my life has been filled with circles, with important events and work and people reappearing, in 1993 I received a call in my office at the United Nations in Geneva saying that the attorney general of Ethiopia would like to meet with me. He told me that Ethiopia wanted to prosecute people from the former regime of dictator Mengistu Haile Mariam, who had been in power for almost 15 years and whose regime had killed close to 1,000,000 civilians, but did not know exactly what to prosecute the regime for. When I mentioned the Ethiopian penal code of 1957 and its provisions on genocide and crimes against humanity, he said he had never heard of it. I was able to loan him a copy, and to my surprise Ethiopia began to prosecute people in the Mengistu regime for crimes against humanity and genocide. (When the copy of the code was returned to me many years later, after the trials, it was stamped 'Property of the Office of the Special Prosecutor'.) So the 1957 work on a penal code resulted in a series of lengthy trials, culminating in the 2006 conviction of Mengistu in absentia and others in his brutal regime. Of course, as a law student in 1957, I had no idea that such things would come to pass. I was just pleased to have the opportunity to gain experience and be exposed to the drafting process and the concept of the three crimes.[15]

In response to the challenge put to me by Paul Guggenheim, I wrote my paper (in French) justifying the nationalisation of the Suez Canal grounded on a theory called *l'acte illicite*, which was central to all the French literature at the time. (I later translated it to English, and it was my first law review article, published in the *DePaul Law Review Journal* in 1965.)

After receiving my submission, Guggenheim called me to his office. He completely disagreed with everything I had written, he said, but as a jurist, I had done a good job defending an indefensible condition – and he was giving me the highest grade in the class.

Choosing my words with care and apologising if I was misspeaking, I told Guggenheim that he was an honourable man who had taught me an important lesson. I said I had been concerned that because he was a Jew and because he had argued against Egypt's nationalisation of the canal, he would be biased against me.

---

[15] I helped draft these same three provisions against genocide, crimes against humanity, and war crimes for the ICTY in 1993, and, after that, in 1998 in the draft of the ICC statute.

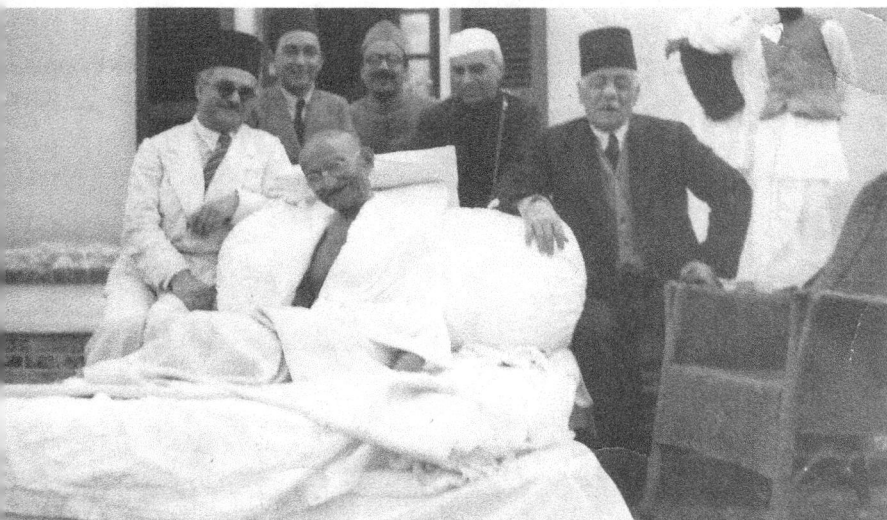

My paternal grandfather's quest to meet Mahatma Gandhi and show Egypt's support r India's independence movement ended in Gujarat, India. From left, three Egyptian ssociates of my grandfather, Jawaharlal Nehru, and my grandfather Mahmoud Bassiouni rround Gandhi.

My parents and I were photographed in October 1938 for my first diplomatic passport.

3. While my parents were living in New York, in my earliest years I was primarily raised by women, including two of my nannies shown in this photograph from the late 1930s.

4. My adoring mother, Amina Khattab, and me in Egypt in the late 1930s.

5. Posing with a traditional Egyptian fez in Egypt in the early to mid-1940s.

6. After my father was posted to Brazil as an Egyptian consul general, he and my mother and I traveled from Brazil to New York City by boat in 1947. Here my father and I relax on deck somewhere in the Atlantic Ocean.

7. Smiling for the camera sometime in the 1940s.

8. With my school classmates in Egypt in the 1940s. I am in the second row from the top, the sixth student from the left.

9. Although my finances were very limited during my time in Dijon, France, in the early 1950s, I much enjoyed socializing and dining with my law school classmates.

10. In 1956, wearing my military uniform, surrounded by family members in Egypt.

11. Ready to ride outside my uncle's house in Cairo in the late 1950s.

12 and 13. My second cousin, Maj. Gen. Abdel Moneim Riad, who became one of Egypt's military leaders, strongly opposed my joining the military, but I was able to become a member of the National Guard and wore its uniform proudly in this 1956 photo in Cairo.

14. Law school graduation day, August 1964, in Indianapolis, Indiana.

15. On vacation with my mother in Europe in the mid-1960s.

16. At a press conference with Egyptian President Anwar Sadat in the 1970s in Egypt.

17. Working in my office at the Siracusa Institute for Criminal Justice and Human Rights in the late 1970s in Siracusa, Italy.

18. With my father, Ibrahim Bassiouni, in Egypt in the mid-1970s.

19. At the airport in Sarajevo, standing in front of the flag of the United Nations Protection Forces, known as UNPROFOR, in April 1993. The banner displays all the flags of the states that contributed troops to UNPROFOR missions.

20. When focusing on issues concerning the former Yugoslavia, I often worked out of my United Nations office in Geneva.

1. In April 1993, I was sleeping when mortar shells began to fall and destroyed the room next to mine at the Holiday Inn in Sarajevo.

2. The conference that produced the Rome Statute opened in June 1998. I am seated second from the left, listening to UN Secretary-General Kofi Annan address conference attendees.

23. At Il Campidoglio, during the ceremony for the opening of the Rome Statute for signature, I am flanked by (from left) Hans Corell, Philippe Kirsch, Giovanni Conso, and Roy Lee.

Prof. Benjamin Ferencz, Prof. Cherif Bassiouni, President Robinson, H.E. Philippe Kirsch, Mr. Hans Corell

Trinidad & Tobago

H.E. President Arthur N.R. Robinson, T.C., O.C.C., S.C.

$2·50

Commemorating the Inauguration of the International Criminal Court

24. This stamp from Trinidad & Tobago was created to celebrate the inauguration of the International Criminal Court. From left, Benjamin Ferencz, me, President of Trinidad & Tobago Arthur N. R. Robinson, Philippe Kirsch, and Hans Corell.

25. In New York in February 1999, I presented UN Secretary-General Kofi Annan with a copy of my book *The Statute of the International Criminal Court: A Documentary History*.

26. During a challenging meeting with Afghan Chief Justice Fazal Hadi Shinwari, I offered my proposal for the training of 400 Afghani judges. From left, my associate Hatem Ali, me, Chief Justice Shinwari, and one of his associates.

27 and 28. During my time as UN Independent Expert on Human Rights in Afghanistan, I inspected conditions at Pul-e-Charkhi prison outside Kabul in July and August 2004 and again in February 2005.

29. Investigating human rights in Afghanistan included discussions in Kabul with Afghanistan President Hamid Karzai in February 2005 about the continuing violations resulting from inadequate prison conditions.

30. My longtime colleague and close friend Benjamin Ferencz and I, shown here in Florida in 2016, often discussed the future of international criminal justice and human rights.

31. My wife, Elaine, presented me with this sweatshirt, which I wore with much amusement and pride. This photograph was taken in 2011 at our home in Michigan.

Guggenheim then talked about leaving Nazi Germany in 1932. He said that in 1943, a very small group of Jews at Auschwitz had managed to escape and brought back reports of the horrors of the concentration camps, stories that prompted Guggenheim and a number of people from the Jewish Agency to travel to Switzerland to meet with Allen Dulles, brother of then-Secretary of State John Foster Dulles. Allen Dulles was the first director of the Central Intelligence Agency (CIA); at the time, he was the representative of the Office of Strategic Services (OSS), the predecessor to the CIA. Guggenheim said he and his colleagues told Allen Dulles about the Auschwitz escapees' accounts of how the Nazis were exterminating people in the camp, and asked that the American air force bombard the railroad tracks leading to Auschwitz.

With great sadness, the kind that comes from knowing that human interest is sometimes deemed less important than military interest, Guggenheim told me he later learned that the US government had refused, saying that the concentration camps were not strategic targets. How could aircraft be deployed to destroy rail routes to a factory or a military camp – but not be used to prevent the tragedies of the concentration camps, even after testimony from eyewitnesses like the man I saw with my father in Cairo all those years ago?

In 1945, Guggenheim had gone back to the US government, again with representatives from the Jewish Agency, with a petition to have the United States take in 10,000 German Jewish children, all under the age of 12, who had been hidden from the Nazis and had foster homes in the United States ready for them. Dulles passed the information on to President Harry Truman, and the administration introduced special legislation to amend the immigration laws to let in the 10,000 children. The House Committee on Immigration, however, refused to even consider the bill, a decision widely attributed to the anti-Semitism of the time. But to distance itself from the embarrassment, the US State Department asked the various petitioners to complete the immigration papers, and so an enormous amount of paperwork was completed for the 10,000 applicants. The applications were rejected, however, because they lacked certificates affirming that the applicants had no prior criminal records, documents obtainable only from German police stations. On this flimsy basis, the children were denied the opportunity to be in the United States legally.

These stories broke my heart, but Guggenheim's and my conversation created a rapport. He respected my principled position for Egypt and welcomed my sympathy for and understanding of what had happened to the Jews. 'In an ideal world', he said, 'principled positions like yours, fighting imperialism and colonialism, would be married to positions like mine, because both of them stem from a respect for human dignity.'

***

I first heard the words *cour penal international*, or international criminal court, in 1957, when I was a 20-year-old student in another seminar at the University of Geneva law school, listening to a lecture by Jean Graven, the former president of the university who at the time was dean of the law school.

My first personal hands-on encounter with an attempt to establish an international criminal court came more than two decades later, in 1979, when I was asked by the UN Ad Hoc Committee for Southern Africa to prepare a draft statute for the establishment of an international criminal court to prosecute violations of the Apartheid Convention. While no action was taken on the statute for political reasons, the proposal I drafted was not in vain because it served as a model for future draft statutes and the task gave me my first taste of what it might be like to bring the idea of an international criminal court to fruition.

1989–1998 and 2002: New York, Siracusa and Rome

ALTHOUGH I NEVER ceased thinking, writing or debating about the establishment of an international criminal court, it wasn't until about ten years later that I had another chance to be intimately involved in the establishment of such a court. This time it was the beginning of a long and arduous but ultimately successful path.

Like many good things in life, this part of my journey began with a phone call from a longtime friend, Arthur N. R. Robinson, then prime minister and later president of Trinidad and Tobago. It was November 1989, and Robinson asked if we could get together in New York, where he was staying for the meeting of the UN General Assembly's Sixth Committee, the primary forum for the consideration of legal questions in the General Assembly.

Robinson told me that during the meeting his country's permanent representative to the United Nations was going to introduce a resolution requesting that the General Assembly put the question of establishing an international criminal court to prosecute drug trafficking before the International Law Commission (ILC), which had been established to study and promote international law initiatives.

Trinidad and Tobago's strategic proposal worked, and a resolution was adopted by the General Assembly's Sixth Committee requesting that the ILC examine the matter. My connection with Dean Graven paid off again as the AIDP, which Graven had introduced me to many years before, was also focusing on the creation of an international criminal court. The AIDP assembled a committee of experts to draft a statute for an international criminal court that would have jurisdiction over all international crimes, and I was invited to chair the panel.

The committee soon gathered at the Siracusa Institute to work, and the draft statute we produced was modelled on my 1981 proposal prepared under Article 5 of the Apartheid Convention. This draft went through a number of reviews by various UN committees and a host of experts, while other drafts on the same topic, prepared by other expert groups, including the ILC, did the same. Those of us determined to help bring about the establishment of a permanent international criminal court were taking many different avenues and working toward our shared goal in a variety of ways. Although the initial directive by the General Assembly was to produce a statute for an international criminal court limited to drug trafficking, the United Nations and the international community looked favourably on the work done on a statute without such limitation. By 1995, the UN established the Ad Hoc Committee for the Establishment of an International Criminal Court, of which I was the vice-chair. I was very involved in the next series of steps by the Preparatory Committee on the Establishment of an International Criminal Court, known as PrepCom. PrepCom's work was well received by the General Assembly and continued through 1997. The General Assembly finally called for a conference, and all our work came to a head in that 1998 conference in Rome on the topic of establishing what is now known as the International Criminal Court.

Those of us who were involved well understood how much work needed to be done, and done quickly, to guarantee that the conference would be a success. Many of us wanted to be sure that the court we were trying to establish would be the product of all states, not just Western or wealthy nations, and I particularly focused on ensuring that representatives from developing and least-developed countries, known as LDCs, could contribute to our work before, during and after the conference. To help alleviate some of the significant travel and accommodation costs, the United Nations established a trust fund to help LDCs have one delegate per applying country. Through the funding of the John D. and Catherine T. MacArthur Foundation, a similar assistance programme was established at DePaul University, and these two funds helped bring many LDC delegates to PrepCom sessions as well as the Rome Conference. My own assistants helped arrange the travel and accommodation for the representatives, making sure they arrived safely in Rome and had no logistical problems there. As a result, many LDCs, many of which were African nations, could fully participate in the drafting and passing of what came to be known as the Rome Statute. This was crucial, as African nations still make up the largest block of parties to the statute. Senegal, in fact, was the first state in the world to ratify the treaty.

In preparing for the Rome Conference, we continued the work of PrepCom, which was focused on drafting a statute to be debated and adopted in Rome, as the four-week conference in Italy would not offer nearly enough time to produce a treaty on such a complicated topic. By the beginning of April 1998, just two months before the conference was to begin, we had a draft text – but it was 173 pages long and included 116 articles with 1,300 words in brackets.

As is so often the case, the road to Rome was not without obstacles. Because we barely had time to edit the final text and translate it from English into the other official UN languages, most governments received translated copies in late April (and some even in early June), just before the conference was to open. This meant that some states had only six weeks to ensure that their respective foreign affairs, justice, and in some cases, defence ministries received the text. When we arrived in Rome, we learned that the many states' foreign affairs ministries had not communicated with their justice ministries until the last minute, so they were unable to adequately prepare for the conference and its discussions. Some states excluded their justice or defence ministries altogether and involved only their ministries of foreign affairs, all of which meant that delegations had little time to examine the text or to get specific instructions for the conference negotiations.

Complicating matters was the reality that until this point, the establishment of an international criminal court had meant very little to those outside the international criminal law field, including even governments and public officials, and this limited consideration hampered some negotiations before and during the conference.

The conference opened on 15 June 1998, with an air of excitement as well as apprehension. At the start, about 5,000 delegates from more than 160 nations were in attendance, although that number shrank to about 2,000 by the end of the first week, as many could not stay for the entire conference. The opening speaker, UN Secretary-General Kofi Annan, closed his powerful message to the thousands gathered in Rome with the following challenge:

> We have before us an opportunity to take a monumental step in the name of human rights and the rule of law. We have an opportunity to create an institution that can save lives and serve as a bulwark against evil ... to bequeath to the next century a powerful instrument of justice. Let us rise to the challenge. Let us give succeeding generations this gift of hope. They will not forgive us if we fail.

With those words in our minds, we moved forward in our tremendous undertaking.

The conference itself was filled with challenges. As soon as I entered the building housing the conference, the headquarters of the Food and Agriculture Organization of the United Nations, I knew some logistics would be even more difficult than we had expected. The building had more than 100 meeting rooms, only three of which were permanently designated, to the Committee of the Whole, the Working Group, and the

Drafting Committee. This meant that when the meeting rooms assigned to informal working groups were changed without much notice, as often happened, delegates struggled to find them. The building's layout, three horizontal wings connected by vertical corridors, added to the confusion. (The layout did provide one unexpected benefit, when those of us on the Drafting Committee were assigned to the Malaysia Room, named for the nation that had donated its furnishings, which was in building C on the second floor, far from the Committee of the Whole and other areas that the media knew about. As a result, we were able to work without interruption or attention.) The lack of air conditioning in the majority of the meeting rooms also made working conditions less than comfortable during an extremely hot and humid Rome summer.

We soon found a logistical challenge of even greater concern: translation. Just three days into the conference, we learned that the text we produced in English each day, which was translated into the other official UN languages overnight, was being sent to various translators in Geneva and New York. This unusual process was intended to save money (by not having to cover the transportation and accommodation costs of having translators on site), but it led to unexpected and frustrating results. With different translators working on different articles and, as was often the case, different translators working on different paragraphs of the same articles, translations had little consistency. Given the already contentious and difficult negotiations over the exact language of certain articles, this was not good.

Attempting to solve this problem, I asked that all the delegates serving on the Drafting Committee rearrange their seating by linguistic affinity rather than by alphabetical order (as is UN protocol). The linguistic groups then worked together to review the translated texts, comparing translations to ensure that all the texts reflected the same meaning. This process was not easy, but it worked.

First we clarified the meaning of a term or concept in the text in English, and then we determined its equivalent in the five remaining UN languages: Arabic, Chinese, French, Russian and Spanish. Sometimes, because of the care with which diplomatic terms had been chosen, we were unable to reconcile the different legal concepts; in those instances, we contacted the relevant working group so its members could try to clarify the ambiguities in the text. Several times we were able to come to a resolution on the ambiguities, but sometimes we could not. This approach to the question of translation resulted in the Drafting Committee's taking on the responsibility of both translation and review. Once we had completed our translations, the UN reviewers examined the translations, and they were then sent back to the Drafting Committee for a final reading.

We were able to find some humour in our work. One involved Article 3 of the Rome Statute, which in English reads, 'The seat of the Court shall be established at The Hague in the Netherlands …'. When we were reviewing the translation of that provision, a Chinese delegate read the text and immediately said, 'No, no. That cannot be.'

When I asked what the problem was, he quietly said that the Chinese translation read 'The butt of the Court …'. We all had a good chuckle and moved on.

The delegates' varied levels of preparedness posed another big challenge. After the first week, the remaining attendees fell into two groups, those who had worked on or studied the draft statute we had started the conference with, and those who had little or no knowledge of it.

The first group, the ones who knew something about the proposed text, accounted for only about 10 per cent of those present, and for the most part we were optimistic about our ability to succeed in establishing an international criminal court. The rest, the majority, were not optimistic. At the onset of the conference, many raised issues and questions that had already been debated, at times even settled, by PrepCom, a phenomenon that by the second week caused some delegates to wonder whether we would need a second diplomatic conference to resolve all the issues.

The slow pace and accompanying pessimism of the conference's first two weeks spurred Philippe Kirsch, the chairman of the Committee of the Whole (more practically, the head of the conference) to organise a number of informal working groups, which organically broke down into about a dozen smaller informal working groups. Delegations also began to consult and worked in regional and political groups. In particular, the Arab states became a very active informal group, meeting frequently and adopting common positions, often ones that were not in support of the establishment or operation of an international criminal court.

Of all these informal groups, the group of 'like-minded states',[16] which at the start of the diplomatic conference included Australia, Austria, Argentina, Belgium, Canada, Chile, Croatia, Denmark, Egypt, Finland, Germany, Greece, Guatemala, Hungary, Iceland, Ireland, Lesotho, the Netherlands, New Zealand, Norway, Portugal, Samoa, Slovakia,

---

[16] Many benefits arose from the presence of the group of 'like-minded states', including the group's willingness to hear the positions of NGOs on various matters, which allowed states that were not a part of the group to participate in meetings and discussions.

South Africa, Sweden, Switzerland, Trinidad and Tobago (representing 12 Caricom states), Uruguay and Venezuela, met the most frequently and focused on coming to positions of compromise on the actual text of the statute. The like-minded states, which had been in existence as early as 1995, really became the driving force behind the passage of the statute at the conference.

These small-group meetings, though necessary to accomplish all the work ahead, forced many delegates to work 10- to 12-hour days, and those of us who were in leadership positions worked even longer hours. The complexity of the issues, the lack of effective negotiating on the more difficult provisions of the statute, and the long workdays did nothing to diminish the growing pessimism of the delegates. These difficulties especially affected the smaller delegations at the conference, as many had only two or three members and therefore could not attend all the meetings taking place at any one time. This was also the case for the UN Secretariat, which did not have enough staff and had to send law student interns to some small-group meetings. There were other difficulties: because we had no simultaneous interpretation of spoken words (as another cost-saving measure), all the meetings were conducted in English, which put non-English-speaking delegations at a severe disadvantage.

The working-group arrangement fulfilled its intended goal of speeding the process, but it exacerbated another issue: attendees approached the statute articles piecemeal, not as a whole, which was particularly frustrating for someone who had been involved in the drafting process for decades. The delegates who attended the entire conference and engaged in the issues had received differing degrees of specificity in instructions from their governments. From my own observations throughout the conference, I thought that delegates from developed countries arrived with specific and detailed instructions, while most of those from least-developed countries, which typically had smaller delegations, had received comparatively vague and limited instructions. This meant that because delegations from developed countries had broader discretionary authority, more specific instructions and larger delegations, they could participate fully in negotiations, while others, perhaps concerned about opposition from senior officials in their home countries, had to be more restrained.

By 5 July 1998, the work of the conference had slowed to the point where our chances of success were in serious jeopardy. With only two weeks left, we still had to address a number of major issues in the text. With a potential breakdown on the horizon, Philippe Kirsch had a

'Chairman's Paper' produced that dealt with what he saw as the major issues that had been unresolved before the conference began, in the hope that this would refocus the delegates and give them a draft compromise. Although the paper did prompt discussions, it did not lead to the negotiations Kirsch and others hoped for, in part because various countries staked out inflexible positions. Officials gave various reasons for these stances, including instructions from their respective governments. This was true of the United States, despite many accommodations made to the statute to appease US representatives, including some involving procedure and definitions of crimes. The United States had previously conceded on certain points such as the court's jurisdiction and the independent role of the prosecutor, but at the conference itself, the delegates adopted unyielding positions on those issues.

The Drafting Committee, which I chaired, had its own challenges, largely stemming from the use of small, informal working groups. Every day our committee received a few completed articles from the Committee of the Whole, along with some 10–15 draft paragraphs from other various articles throughout the draft statute.[17] Because we got these draft paragraphs, our own version of puzzle pieces, periodically rather than receiving all the paragraphs for one article at once, completing the jigsaw puzzle that was the draft statute was extremely difficult as we struggled to ensure the continuity and clarity of the draft statute amid the wide variety of the working groups' legal approaches, languages and drafting techniques.

Despite all these obstacles and challenges throughout our five weeks of work, we completed all 111 articles of the draft statute by 15 July 1998. Some issues of text and process did remain, and these ultimately

---

[17] The process by which the text of the articles moved through the working groups and informal meetings was as follows. A working group would submit a draft provision to the Committee of the Whole for pro forma approval. The Committee of the Whole then examined each new textual provision, after which the provision was labelled 'rolling text' and put to the side until the committee received the rest of the articles in which they belonged. When the Committee of the Whole had received the full text of an article, it would go to the Secretariat. The Secretariat would then prepare a separate document of the text and assign it a conference symbol number, and then the text would be translated and sent to the Drafting Committee for review. Then the Drafting Committee would review and discuss the text and label the articles 'text adopted on first reading'. The Drafting Committee then waited for the rest of the text of the draft statute to determine whether the language of each given article was consistent with the statute as a whole. After such determination was made, the Drafting Committee labelled the article 'text adopted on second reading'. Once the Drafting Committee completed an entire part of the draft statute, it reported to the Committee of the Whole.

led to inconsistencies or ambiguity in the draft statute, but such things were to be expected in light of our monumental task. The majority of these issues were political in nature, such as the court's relationship with the UN Security Council and the definition of crimes, and were located in what was referred to as Part 2 of the draft statute. These provisions were heavily debated for the last two weeks of the conference, and it was not until the very last day of the conference, 17 July, that the proposed text of Part 2 was submitted to the Committee of the Whole. Part 2 was submitted with the stipulation that it be accepted or rejected in its entirety, a move that was highly controversial. But at such a late stage, any additional debate on Part 2 would probably have caused the conference to collapse. All we could do was hope for the best.

Although the conference was scheduled to conclude at 6 pm on 17 July, we weren't quite done with our work, so we came to an unspoken agreement that we would extend the conference until 11:59 pm. Even with the extra hours, however, we soon realised that if we hoped to leave Rome with an adopted statute, we would need to work well into the morning of 18 July. As the clock ticked closer to midnight during the night of 17 July, I stopped what I was doing, went over to the clock, took it off the wall and removed its batteries. We continued with the work at hand and, in a way, finished before the conference's official end.

As midnight on 17 July approached, the United States and India sought to introduce last-minute amendments to the text of Part 2. Luckily, Norway responded by introducing a no-action motion, which in practice is a motion to table, to each of the motions, and Kirsch, in accordance with the conference rules, gave voting precedent to the no-action motions. The votes in favour of two no-action motions were overwhelming, and with that, Part 2 was adopted and our work was largely done. After the second vote in favour of the no-action motion, the room burst into applause that lasted close to ten minutes. After five weeks of long days and hard work at the conference (and for many of us, after years of work on the topic), we had achieved success. Delegates hugged each other, cheering, crying tears of joy (and possibly exhaustion). It was the most emotional scene I have ever witnessed in a diplomatic setting.

After the Committee of the Whole had taken its final vote it adjourned, and shortly afterwards, the Plenary opened its final session. We had expected this last session to be a quick and formal one before the conference was officially closed, but in a move that surprised all of us, the United States asked for another vote, a move I assumed was meant to encourage some states to vote against the statute. But when the Plenary held its formal final vote, the delegations from 120 countries voted to adopt the statute. Although 21 countries abstained from the vote and 7 countries, including the United States, voted against the statute, the results were clear: we had the framework to establish the International Criminal Court. The world was ready for the institution that had been on my mind since I had been a young man in Geneva. To say I was ecstatic would be a dramatic understatement.

After the overwhelmingly positive vote, we allowed for post-vote statements by delegates that stretched past 2 am on 18 July. A few hours later all the delegates gathered again, this time a bit more rested and dressed for photographers. The Secretariat and internationally located translators finalised the text, which was completed in time for a 4 pm gathering at Il Campidoglio[18] for the formal opening of the statute. Within about two hours of the statute being opened for signature, 26 states had signed onto it.

What is now commonly called the Rome Statute remained in Rome at the Italian Ministry of Foreign Affairs, available for signature, until 30 October 1998, when it traveled to the UN headquarters in New York and was deposited with the secretary-general. After so many years of work by so many people, we were stunned to learn that by 21 December 2000, the last day that states could sign on to the statute (after that, they could only accede to it), 139 had signed on. Signing on was only the first step; states still had to ratify the statute through their own domestic processes before they could officially become parties to the statute, but this was great success in a short time.

In the next two years, the necessary 60 states ratified the statute, allowing it to enter into force and for the International Criminal Court, known as the ICC, to be physically and conceptually established. My colleagues and I finally had the chance to see our dream become a reality.

Although this enormous accomplishment brought me joy, it came with some personal disappointments, including knowing that for the foreseeable future, I could never be intimately involved in the day-to-day operations of the institution. In drafting the Rome Statute, we stipulated that every individual nominated as a judge, as well as other positions, must be a national of a state party to the court. By the time it was clear that the court would be established and begin its judicial work, the United States had indicated that it would probably never become a state party to the court. In the back of my mind I had long hoped that I could be appointed as a judge at the ICC, a role I always envisioned myself

---

[18] Rome's city hall, designed by Michelangelo to be the seat of the Roman Senate.

filling through my Egyptian citizenship. Unfortunately, at the time the first class of judges was appointed, Egypt had not ratified the Rome Statute and did not appear likely to do so in the near future. (I also could not be sure that even if it did become a state party, Egypt would nominate me.) Egypt still has not become a party to the ICC, so my dream of serving as a judge for the institution I helped create was never realised.

August 1957–April 1958:
Alexandria and Cairo

IN 1957, AFTER the law school quarter ended in Geneva, my father asked me to come back to Egypt. He said that the Ministry of Foreign Affairs wanted to talk to me about what happened in France, which was understandable. What I did not know was that when Wahid Ramadan returned to Egypt after issuing his report highly critical of Sarwat Okasha, he had been arrested and tortured by the Egyptian GIA.

When my ship arrived in Alexandria, my father and his business manager were waiting at the port, along with two men from the GIA, which is responsible for providing national security intelligence domestically and transnationally. I did not know who the men were, but upon arrival I got the royal treatment: my passport was stamped, I did not have to go through customs and I had no hassles. The men from the GIA made sure that I would be in Cairo within the next day or so to talk to them. I thought that I was a hero and that they were going to give me fitting treatment. From this innocuous beginning, my saga with the GIA spiralled beyond my imagination, down into a pit of desperation.

* * *

None of what occurred during my house arrest was official. There were never any legal proceedings, legal orders or official records. No charges, no court orders, nothing. It was all pure and simple extrajudicial abuse of power. And it was all set off quite abruptly.

I spent a day or two with my father at his apartment in Alexandria before making my way to Cairo for my promised meeting with the two intelligence officers to discuss, I believed, my arrest and detainment by French authorities. By this time, I was living in the family apartment in Cairo, as my mother had left Egypt and was living with her new husband, an American, in Indianapolis.

The place where I had agreed to meet the GIA men turned out to be an annexe in the office of the presidency in Abdin Palace, where some of the officers were at work. The man I met said he was a captain, though he did not say which agency he was in. To this day, I do not know if he was working for Military Intelligence or the GIA. The captain did his best to befriend me, as did his brother, an attorney who had worked for Military Intelligence or the GIA, although once again I did not know which one. I had no qualms about meeting with the men because they gave me the impression that I was being screened to serve on President Nasser's staff. Despite my youth, I had had some occasion to interact with the top tier of the military and government; in sum, I was not without hubris. I was frequenting the office of the presidency, imagining that those I was talking with were evaluating me for a job.

Then the captain showed me a photograph, and my life changed. It was the second week of August 1957, in the captain's office in Abdin Palace, when he showed me a picture of a torture victim, a man strapped in a chair with a metal band around his head. The band had a screw, and where the screw had been turned, you could see brain matter. This, the captain told me, was a leader of the Muslim Brotherhood, the Sunni Islamist group founded in Egypt in 1928.

I could barely keep it together after seeing such a gruesome image. About the time I finally composed myself, the hallway outside erupted with noise, another man entered the captain's office, and the captain slid the photograph into his desk drawer. The presidential meeting had been cancelled, the second man said, so the vice-president would be meeting with a few senior officials.

One of the two vice-presidents at the time was Kamaluddin Hussein, who during the 1956 war had been the commander for the Suez Canal area and, therefore, technically my commander-in-chief. I had seen him only once, at the ceremony where I received the medal of military merit for my service in the Suez.

Still stunned by the photograph I had just seen, I was further surprised when the captain asked whether I would like to meet the vice-president. I said yes, though I had met him before. Then I said the first thing that came to my mind – I was not a member of the Muslim Brotherhood. I had never been part of it and had no sympathy for its political aims.

The captain and I joined a group of staff members who greeted the vice-president when he stepped out of a lift. After saluting, the captain introduced me as a second lieutenant who had just returned from France, where I had been in prison.

The vice-president turned, looked at me, and said, 'Don't I know you?'

When I said I had met him at the awards ceremony, all the military personnel nearby hastened to show their attention and respect. *'Ibni'*

(My son), many exclaimed in the typical paternalism that often marks the military order. The vice-president then put his arm around my shoulder and dragged me down the hallway to the meeting room.

As other people flowed into the room, the vice-president introduced me to each one, letting everyone know that I had commanded the first Egyptian line of defence against the British at Port Said. I was the centre of attention, praised for my role in the war and admired for being arrested in France because of training the Algerians. The vice-president asked me why I was there, and without thinking, I said I was probably being considered for a position in the president's office. He responded kindly.

But I persisted. 'I have to tell you something', I said. 'Will you please tell the president that people are being tortured in prisons. Do you know this is being done in the name of the government, in the name of the revolution, and this is illegal?'

One sentence was all it took. Still less than 20 years old, I was so idealistic, perhaps just naïve, that I thought President Nasser did not know about the torture and that the government could never knowingly engage in such abuses.

When the vice-president pressed me for details, I told him about the photograph I had just seen. People, I said, must be doing this without the knowledge of the president and the revolutionaries because torture was surely not something they would condone.

Everyone in the room fell silent. A deputy chief of intelligence, armed and dressed in military uniform, shouted '*Al ikhras!*' He hurled the phrase, which means a mute, someone who cannot speak, at me, intimidation via insult. The man was telling me to become a silent or silenced person. All my emotions boiled over – my nervousness from the vice-president's presence, my revulsion and horror at the photograph of the torture victim, my repressed dread from the episode in France. Everything hit me at once. I lost it.

'You don't tell me *ikhras*! You *ikhras*! [Shut up!]', I exploded, the temper I surely inherited from my mother overwhelming me.

The deputy chief of intelligence drew his gun, and pandemonium broke out. Two military officers came running, twisted my arms behind my back, pulled me out of the room and pushed me into another. I was told that the decision hadn't yet been made whether I would be shot or tortured, just as the man in the photograph had been.

I was forced to stay in that room for what felt like an eternity, though it was probably no more than a few hours. I tried but could not quell my agitation. I was tormented. I was afraid. I just could not seem to catch my breath. I must have died a thousand times in those hours. Not one rational thought entered my mind as I was trapped in that room, my future unknown.

Eventually an intelligence officer appeared, put me in handcuffs, and took me down the hall, onto the elevator, out of the building and into the back of a police car. My passport, which I had presented to enter the palace, was taken from me. The officer then drove me to my house, parked the car, removed my handcuffs and let me out of the car. Two other police officers in civilian clothes, already waiting outside my apartment building, escorted me to my door. Then they told me the rules of the captivity that would last seven months.

* * *

'You cannot see anyone. You cannot talk to anyone. You cannot leave your apartment. Nothing, until we tell you so.' That was it. My window shutters were nailed closed. My radios were removed, and my telephone confiscated. Two guards were stationed at one door to my apartment, two guards at the other door and one guard was stationed at the door to my kitchen. Just like that, I was a prisoner in my own home.

That first night I did not even pretend I could sleep. I turned on every light in the apartment and just sat trembling, without any idea about what to do. As the sun crept through the slats of the shutters, I realised that for the first time I was no longer in control of my own life. While there had been times when I had been forced to do what others said, including when I was at boarding school and in the military, this was different. I felt as if I were treading water, just trying to stay afloat, unable to swim and terrified of drowning.

When the back door of my apartment opened early that first morning, terror engulfed me. I froze. I heard noises in the kitchen and then the sound of the door closing. On the kitchen table I later found a pot of tea, two loaves of bread, some cheese and some *foul*, a dish made from fava beans that many Egyptians start their day with. I instinctively knew that this would be the routine. After a few days, the food began arriving twice daily.

That first afternoon of my house arrest, fear so paralysed me I could not even force myself to walk down the hallway between my bedroom and living room. I was so afraid of what would face me, what would come out from behind the windows, behind the shadows, behind everything. Never since have I been so afraid. I kept all the lights on at night because I could not handle shadows. I jumped at the slightest noise.

By the next day, I was able to walk from my bedroom to the kitchen to get food and go to the bathroom. My fear never subsided, but I forced myself to push through it. That first week, I mostly stayed in my bedroom, and even in the weeks that followed, I spent most of my time curled up in the fetal position on my bed. (Decades later, I sometimes found myself falling asleep in the same position.)

The only thing I was able to focus on was the Qur'an. I had a few religious books as well, and during this time I fell deep into mysticism. In fact, when it was all over, I joined a Sufi group and became a kind of mystic over the next three years. I could not deal with a reality over which I had no control, a reality where some force that I recognised to be evil had all the power. It was the epitome of inhumanity, and I couldn't deal with it. I fluctuated between seeking solace in faith and rebelling against God for the existence of that evil – how could you allow it, God? – not because it was happening to me but because it existed at all. How could God accept people who are doing such evil to others? My anger was almost depersonalised, detached as I was from the world.

I cannot begin to describe my fear of being tortured. The guards never tried to question me during that period, but their inaction was punitive. Police officers visited me only twice. One I will never forgive. He had a beautiful smile and very nice manners, and he asked, 'What would you like most?'

'What I would like most is if I could just die', I said.

He reached into his pocket, pulled out a bullet, and put it on the table. 'This is worth one piaster', he said, referring to the coin worth 1/100th of the Egyptian pound. 'You want to tell me your life is worth one piaster?'

'If that bullet could go into my head now, it would be worth a million.'

'Well', he said, 'that bullet is not going to go into your head. But maybe one day you will go to that place where the photograph of the man whose brain was squeezed out of his head was taken. We haven't made up our mind yet whether you're worth a piaster or whether we should send you there to taste what he died of.'

That sent me back to the catatonic state, back to the fetal position. My fear of torture was so overwhelming that at that point, I would have done anything to kill myself or die.

During my house arrest, only two men were allowed to enter my apartment other than the guards and police. Haj Abdul Hamid, my dear and trusted business manager and in many ways my guide and mentor, was allowed to visit me only because he pushed his way in at considerable risk and peril. After a while my family's cook, Usta Mohammad Mustafa, was also allowed to come into the apartment to cook and clean, although the guard at the kitchen door checked his entry and exit, along with everything he brought into or took out of the apartment.

Because the guards wore civilian clothes, no one could tell their purpose. In some ways, however, their number was impressive: as anyone in the security field knows, a round-the-clock detail of five is both unusual and expensive. The person being guarded must be particularly important or particularly threatening to something – or someone – in the regime.

After seven months of my house arrest, Haj Abdul Hamid came to see me one day in the early evening and on his way in was approached by one of the two security men at the building's entrance. After surprising Haj Abdul Hamid with the customary greeting *al-salamu 'alaikum*, the guard said, as casually as if he were talking about the weather, 'Why doesn't the *uztaz* [an honorific used generically for any man considered learned, including attorneys] Bassiouni go out for a walk during the day to get some fresh air.'

Haj Adbul Hamid, who was a cool character, very poised, very temperate, and a man of few words, responded, 'Thank you. I will let him know.'

Haj Abdul Hamid waited to tell me of this exchange until we were on the balcony of my apartment, drinking the tea Usta Mohammad had brought – dark, strong and with a lot of sugar, as Haj Abdul Hamid liked it. After the first two satisfying sips, Haj Abdul Hamid relayed the security man's message. 'I take it they are allowing you out', he said. 'But I would not be more optimistic at this point.'

I was shocked but elated and bombarded Haj Abdul Hamid with questions. He repeated that this was all the man had said; did I want him to go back and ask for more information? When I asked his advice, Haj Abdul Hamid said, as he had so many times before, 'Let's wait and see.'

'And when I leave', he continued, 'I will tell him that you thank his superiors for the decision and that we'll go out for less than an hour tomorrow at, say, 4 in the afternoon. I will walk you in the neighbourhood.'

Did the guards need advance notice before I left the apartment? Haj asked them, and the answer was that I could go as I pleased from 8 am to 8 pm until further notice. I was encouraged but had no idea what had brought about this change. I was operating in the dark, as is standard with security agencies: always keep the person under scrutiny in doubt.

* * *

Leaving my apartment felt like my first day back in the world, like a child's first step. Could it be that my future had been so uncertain that my past had been partially erased? As simple as it sounds, stepping outside was emotionally momentous, as significant for me as Neil Armstrong's step onto the surface of the moon. A small step, but what a giant leap! I had stepped out of confinement and into freedom, albeit a relative freedom. I stepped out of the fear of torture and death into a relative expectation of personal safety.

But the leap was not simple or quick. How many times did I mentally rebel and fight against my fears, only to be overcome and feel crushed again until a wave of rebellion returned, reminding me that I was alive and still my own person? In the end of that process, which took weeks, I often found myself back in my bedroom, back in the fetal position. My emotions were like a yo-yo, especially at night. I felt as if I was going up and down, tethered to someone else's string.

* * *

I was deeply touched that during my darkest moments, two people who had been important throughout my childhood helped me survive: Haj Adbul Hamid and Usta Mohammad Mustafa.

Some of my earliest and fondest childhood memories relate to our chef, Usta Mohammad Mustafa, a Nubian man who started working in my paternal grandfather's house when he was 17 years old. As a small child I called him 'Bakbak'. Back then, my paternal grandfather, Mahmoud Ibrahim Bassiouni, was the president of the Egyptian Senate, and people from his constituency were constantly coming to visit. To accommodate these visitors, my grandfather built a guest house in the garden with a kitchen and four rooms that could house eight guests at a time. People would come from all over the countryside, occasionally bringing with them rice, potatoes or a couple of chickens. Usta Mohammad would organise a menu for them based on what was available in the storage house and what they had brought. If the storage house didn't have enough food, he would use the supplies at the main house. After my parents' divorce, he continued to cook for my mother and then for me, even during my house arrest, until I left Egypt.

When I think back on Usta Mohammad, two things come to mind. The first is the pride that he took in his appearance: even though he worked with food, his clothes were always immaculately washed and ironed. The second is his extraordinary storytelling ability. Like many Egyptians of that time, Usta Mohammad did not know how to read or write, but through an oral tradition of storytelling, our family histories and national stories lived on through his voice.

Usta Mohammad endeared himself to my mother and father because of his love for me and was the only member of the house staff, other than my nurse, who was allowed to hold me. At night, he would come and sit next to my bed, lulling me to sleep with stories of my family, my grandfather, and men and women of the past. His stories, like my own personal Aesop's fables, were never without lessons or messages, and Usta Mohammad became the first formative teacher in my life. He taught me the value of honesty, integrity and loyalty, both through these stories and in the way he conducted himself on a day-to-day basis, feeding people coming from all parts of Upper Egypt.

Haj Abdul Hamid was by my side as I made the transition from child to adult when I took over my family's farm for my father at age 15, and he was my support in the desperate moments of my house arrest. Haj Abdul Hamid, as I referred to him respectfully, first worked for my maternal grandfather, Mohammad Khattab. His father had been the imam of the mosque that my grandfather had built. After finishing grade school, he did two years of an apprenticeship at the religious school but could not pursue his education because his family did not have much money, so he went into farming. Haj Abdul Hamid was always known for his trustworthiness: he was extraordinarily honest and straightforward. The man was as straight as an arrow.

Haj Abdul Hamid learned the trade of being a weigher. When people wanted to purchase a bale of cotton or other farm material, he was the person who weighed the goods. It was a job that required the buyer's trust, and Haj Abdul Hamid's honesty worked well for him. After working as a weigher for some time, he became an accountant in my maternal grandfather's farm, and when my grandfather died, he continued to work for my mother, then for my father, and then for me. When my father had his breakdown and I was forced to take over our family farm, Haj Abdul Hamid stayed, guiding and supporting me.

As a young man, I had plenty of energy and ideas, but it was Haj Abdul Hamid who taught me everything I needed to know about farming. He was my right-hand man – and a trusted and much-needed mentor. I will always be grateful to him for his guidance. His loyalty and kindness never ceased.

April 2004–March 2005: Geneva, Various Cities in Afghanistan

MANY YEARS LATER, long after the passing of my mentor and friend Haj Abdul Hamid, I found myself dealing with torture and imprisonment, though this time I was on the other side of the locked door, serving the United Nations in Afghanistan. Like my own experiences, the plight of these people is not something I could forget.

Despite opposition by the United States to the establishment of such a position and my appointment to it, I was officially named to the role of UN Independent Expert on Human Rights in Afghanistan in April 2004.

I arrived in Kabul on 14 August 2004, ready to dive into my investigation. Luckily for me, the Siracusa Institute, which I was president of at the time, had been conducting judicial trainings in Afghanistan since the summer of the previous year and had access to basic necessities such as housing and transportation. I was forced to rely on the Siracusa Institute for these resources because I received the same amount of funding and support from the United Nations that we had received while conducting our investigation in the former Yugoslavia a decade earlier: none. I depended on the institute not only for the support of its staff but for a place to sleep, cars to travel in and much more.[19]

My first action was to meet with a large number of NGOs and civil society organisations and other organisations to become better informed about human rights violations in the country. It was during these initial meetings, held in Geneva at the end of April 2004, that I first learned about the illegally detained prisoners who would preoccupy much of my time over the next few months. In these meetings I heard that between 3,000 and 4,000 people had been detained by the Northern Alliance in Sheberghan Prison for more than two years in horrible conditions, in

---

[19] I was also extremely fortunate to have the support of the then-UN Secretary-General's Special Representative to Afghanistan, Jean Arnault, who was heading the UN mission in Kabul at the time. He provided me with invaluable political and moral support for the task as well as UN vehicles, without which I could not have safely travelled through the countryside.

what appeared to be a violation of the Geneva Conventions. I spent the next few months reviewing reports on human rights in Afghanistan while also beginning my efforts to secure the freedom of these detainees.

Shortly after I learned of these people's living conditions, I was told that a large number had been released because of health issues, others had been allowed to pay their way out of detention, and 849 had been transferred from the control of the Northern Alliance to the Afghan government at Pul-e-Charkhi prison.

I wrote to the minister of justice of Afghanistan to voice my concerns. In addition to requesting the release of these prisons, I reminded the government of its legal obligations to investigate allegations of torture and other human rights abuses suffered by the detainees and well as the obligation to ensure that the detainees' living conditions met the minimum standards under international law and that the detainees had access to medical services. I received no reply.

During our visit to Pul-e-Charkhi prison, a large facility outside Kabul that is the country's main prison, we quickly saw that conditions were well below international standards. The cells or rooms holding the prisoners were extremely overcrowded, with men packed into small areas for 23 hours a day, forced to sleep and eat together in these spaces. Many of the cells and larger detention rooms that housed the detainees were located on the perimeter of the building, and the windows, and even some of the walls, were made of only metal bars. This meant that those forced to live in these rooms and cells were exposed to the elements, whether it was the intense heat of summer or the freezing cold of winter. The facility's electrical wiring was exposed, creating a serious fire risk. The cells or rooms holding the prisoners were extremely overcrowded; individual cells designed for one person frequently held three or four prisoners, and the larger rooms, which could have housed 40 people, held 60 or more. The prison had no running water or drinking water, and food was scarce.

The facility had no beds; the prisoners slept on the floor in rows, on top of mats and blankets. Each day the prison guards delivered food rations to the prisoners, who then cooked the food in their cells or rooms and distributed it among themselves. The washroom facilities were practically non-existent, and sanitation was deplorable. A large number of those detained were ill, some suffering from highly contagious diseases such as tuberculosis.

We also learned that the prisoners were frequently beaten. I was alerted to this by a note one of the prisoners passed to me. 'To the respected guest', he wrote. 'We have lots of problems here but infront [*sic*] of the security people we cannot complain because when you leave they will beat us. There are beatings going on from the beggining [*sic*]. We have TB patients and this rate is increasing day by day. We have other basic problems but that need [*sic*] explanation and opportunity. From Pakistani prisoners.' This note, along with the deplorable conditions, heightened my determination to see that these men were released.[20]

I thought about the prisoners and their plight constantly, and that night in Kabul I prayed for help getting them out.

The next day, two of my colleagues and I visited Afghani Chief Justice Fazal Hadi Shinwari, whom I had met when conducting judicial training in the country. Speaking in Arabic, I asked whether he had ordered the imprisonment of the men at Pul-e-Charkhi. He said he had not and suggested I talk with the attorney general. (In those days, Shinwari and the attorney general were constantly hurling barbs at each other; the attorney general thought that he was superior to the chief justice because he had a law degree.)

But the attorney general claimed he had no idea why 849 people were in a prison under his jurisdiction. At my request, the attorney general wrote and signed a letter stating that the UN Independent Expert for Human Rights in Afghanistan had notified him about the 849 prisoners, that he had not ordered their imprisonment, and that he in fact had no knowledge of it.

Then I presented the letter to Shinwari, hoping to provoke him because I knew he was very sensitive about his authority. My technique worked: Shinwari was convinced that someone was challenging him, undermining the justice system by running a secret prison system. But who? His initial guess, that the Afghani secret service was working in connection with the CIA, made him even more angry.

---

[20] In addition to my commitment to securing the freedom of these detainees, I was equally determined to investigate allegations of human rights abuses at the hands of US forces, including those alleged to occur at Bagram Air Force Base. To access Bagram, however, I needed to secure permission from US officials, despite my UN mandate, which should have allowed me unrestricted access. In preparation for my first field investigation in Afghanistan in August 2004, the United Nations Assistance Mission in Afghanistan (UNAMA) requested access to Bagram as part of our investigation. But we were given the bureaucratic runaround. Within days we were told by the US Army in Afghanistan that our request needed to be directed to the US Mission to the United Nations in New York, and then we were told that there would probably be a delay in processing the request. We were already on the ground investigating in Afghanistan when we were informed by letter that our request needed to go through the US Permanent Mission in Geneva. Any doubt about whether this back and forth was simply the pitfalls of bureaucracy or an intentional effort to keep me from investigating human rights abuses at Bagram became clear later, when we were prevented from accessing the base on a subsequent field investigation.

Once again I asked for a letter, this one stating that Shinwari had no knowledge of the prisoners' existence, and then presented it, along with the letter from the attorney general, to the minister of the interior. How could so many people be imprisoned without these two men's knowledge?

The minister of the interior said that the US attorney general, John Ashcroft, wanted the prisoners held until they could be interrogated, but he refused to put this in writing. I then went to the US ambassador, Zalmay Khalilzad, and told him I planned to report that the United States had essentially violated the sovereignty of Afghanistan by having the US attorney general order the incarceration of 849 people without any due process and leaving them in miserable conditions.

While I was in his office, Khalilzad telephoned someone and spoke in Pashto, one of Afghanistan's official languages. (Although he correctly assumed that I did not speak Pashto, he didn't know that one of my local collaborators who was with me at the time, an Egyptian, had learned a little of the language.) When he finished his phone conversation, Khalilzad claimed he would look into the situation, but I wasn't satisfied. Without even checking with my Pashto-speaking colleague (who later confirmed that I was correct), I guessed that Khalilzad's phone conversation had been with President Hamid Karzai. I was going to speak directly with Karzai, I told Khalilzad, and an enormous scandal would follow.

President Karzai, who received me because the ambassador had warned him of my visit, swore that he didn't know about the prisoners. Unconvinced, I tried a warning, telling him that if he did not release the prisoners within 30 days, he would be caught up in the biggest scandal he or the Bush administration had ever imagined possible. He might be forced to resign. If he let the men out within a month, I said, I would still document the imprisonment, but in my official report I would make it look as if Karzai had done the right thing.

President Karzai said he would do everything possible to meet the deadline but asked me not to disclose the matter publicly, which I considered an acceptable quid pro quo. I left Karzai, finished my business in Afghanistan and returned to Chicago.

Less than a month later, as I worked on my first report on the situation of human rights in Afghanistan in my Chicago office at DePaul University, I heard that President Karzai had announced that all the prisoners would be released.

I repeated what I had done in my hotel room in Kabul that summer night: I moved to the middle of the room, put my forehead to the ground, and thanked God.

The plight of the detainees was not one I forgot, especially when I went back to Pul-e-Charkhi a few months later and found the remaining prisoners still living in inhumane conditions, this time exposed to brutal cold and snow rather than heat and burning sun.[21]

While I knew that much remained to be done for human rights in Afghanistan and the rest of the world, I was immensely thankful to be able to help those imprisoned and suffering from torture. After my own house arrest and terror in Egypt decades earlier, I was both grateful and in awe of the way the world can work.

* * *

Throughout my time in Afghanistan, I was struck by the condition of women in that country. Wherever I went, I saw that most women were covered from head to toe, and very few were employed or had any right to own property or a business. They were basically commodities for the men in their families – for their fathers, husbands or brothers to dispose of as they please. At that time (and perhaps still, in some places), most young girls were married by the time they reach puberty or shortly thereafter. They had no choice, and once they were in the custody of their husbands, the men could do whatever they wanted with them, including beating and physically mistreating them, unless the girls' families were strong and interested enough to interfere with the spouses' families, which seldom happened. Young girls were frequently given by their families to another family as a kind of compensation.

During the period I was in Afghanistan, from 2003 to 2006, I saw much progress in women's rights, but even so, women in the country's most developed areas are still far from being equal to their counterparts in the West, who have much more opportunity to reach important positions in government, civil society and academia.

My concern about the condition of women was connected to the criminal justice system. In 2003, when I was in Afghanistan for my work with the International Institute of Higher Studies in Criminal Sciences

---

[21] During this second field investigation in Afghanistan, I also visited other detention sites and prisoners, including Logar, where I found the conditions even worse than in Pul-e-Charkhi. In Logar, prisoners were held in cramped metal shipping containers, buried in the ground with very little light, and were inappropriately shackled, in conditions well below the minimum standards required by international law. I made this matter known to Afghani officials and mentioned the conditions in my second, final report on human rights in Afghanistan.

(now known as the Siracusa International Institute for Criminal Justice and Human Rights), I discovered that although a large number of women had been found guilty of serious crimes, there were no women's prisons, and this had serious consequences.

I learned about a case that opened my eyes: a woman about 5 feet 5 inches tall had been found guilty of killing a man who was 6 feet 2 by stabbing him repeatedly in the chest, which to me seemed physically impossible. In fact, her husband had committed the crime, but she had been compelled to confess to a prosecutor and judge and received a 30-year sentence for her husband's crime. Because there was no prison facility for women, she was assigned to the family of the deceased, where she basically became a slave.

I heard about other cases in which men admitted hurting or killing their wives or girlfriends or other men, and instead of punishment, the two families involved would agree on payment of a certain sum of money under Islamic law called *diyya*. This varied from tribe to tribe, but the payment was frequently made in kind by giving young girls in marriage without dowry to the young boys of the aggrieved family. No one knew what became of those girls and women or what the aggrieved family did to them. It was like the end of the world for them, and no one cared. Islam was evoked then, as it is today for other egregious human rights violations, but such things are far from anything that Islam's values would ever encourage.

I convinced the Italian government to build a prison facility for women, but the Ministry of Justice said it lacked resources, and the Italian embassy in Kabul could put together only a small sum. This was enough for a modest building that housed 40 rooms with two bunk beds in each. When I visited the facility, which was run by two Afghani matrons, I thought it seemed a peaceful community, but I was surprised to see the corridors filled with women and children – and then to learn that the children were there because the spouses of the women, most of whom had been imprisoned after falsely confessing to crimes committed by their husband, father or brother, refused to keep them. The children slept on the same bunk beds as their mothers, with only one blanket per bed. The prison received daily food supplies for the 160 female inmates, which meant that the women had to share these with all the children. I tried, unsuccessfully, to get the Afghani government, or any European government, to provide the meagre sum needed to send more food to the prison, but at least I was able to make enough fuss in the United Nations, the European Union and Western embassies to bring some attention to the plight of these women and children.

Men suffered, too: in other provinces, I found that men were often confined, either in some sort of prison or in the custody of the victim's family, and mostly treated as slaves. They were often beaten regularly and poorly fed, with their treatment depending on whether their families would pay ransom.

April 1993–July 1994: The Former Yugoslavia, Geneva, Chicago

D URING THE COMMISSION of Experts' work in the former Yugoslavia, we designed the investigation of rape and sexual crimes so that interviews would be conducted by the female volunteers in teams of three, each with one attorney (in most cases, an attorney with prosecutorial experience), one mental health specialist and one translator. Despite my continued efforts to get the investigation off of the ground, by the end of 1993, a lack of financial support again sent me searching for the funds to move forward.

After delaying the investigation until January 1994 in the hope that the United Nations would finally accept the grant money from the Netherlands and make it available to the commission, I submitted another budget report to the office of Ralph Zacklin, the deputy legal counsel to the UN Office of Legal Affairs, for approval. By now I was not surprised to meet an objection: this time, it was that my budget for the rape investigation was too big. The office informed me that the commission was not allowed to spend what amounted to three-fifths of the total funds, $300,000, on one investigation, even though we all knew that those funds would be covered by the Dutch contribution. In the interests of moving forward, I acquiesced and submitted a new budget, this time totalling only $100,000, which in an investigation that could involve tens of thousands of people amounted to a few dollars per victim. It was approved. (Shortly thereafter, the United Nations accepted the first grant of funding from the Netherlands, which I thought made the entire matter moot.) Once again, it seemed that UN bureaucracy would stop for nobody, not even victims of rape and sexual violence.

* * *

Once we finally received the funds, we moved quickly.[22] This investigation was the first of its kind in many ways, in its immense scale as well as its

---

[22] In addition to the hurdles surrounding the commission's budget, I had to contend with the people in charge of the UN contracts who tried to prevent me from contracting

use of attorneys and mental health specialists. Three days of training for all the volunteers, held in Zagreb in February 1994, included briefings by physicians experienced in dealing with torture victims as well as discussions of the ongoing conflict and other cultural factors that could affect the work. All the prosecutors, most of whom came from common-law countries such as Canada and Australia, had experience prosecuting violent crimes. The psychiatrists and psychologists came from several countries, with the majority hailing from the United States, where many had worked with rape victims suffering from post-traumatic stress. The interpreters were from Croatia, Bosnia and Herzegovina, and Serbia.

Because we knew that many victims would be fearful of retaliation – against them or their families – if they participated in the investigation, we took extra precautions to protect their identities. Each individual we interviewed was first approached by someone not affiliated with the commission or the investigation, which, we believed, allowed us to connect with women we thought would have the most useful information and also not turn away anyone who wanted to speak. This also let the women decide, on their own and without pressure from anyone directly connected with the work, whether they wanted to participate. Finally, this method of connecting with women gave us a way to contact individuals later (such as through the ICTY's Office of the Prosecutor) without having to reveal the subject's identity or location.

All the interviewees' identities were coded, and I alone had access to the key. None of the interviews were taped, and all notes from the interviews were kept in a secure location, accessible only to authorised officials. We were well aware that all those who participated – and also those whose experiences of rape or sexual violence would not be part of our investigation – would have to live with the memories and impact of the traumatic events they had suffered, and we connected with local mental health specialists to ensure immediate and continuing assistance, including medical, psychological, and psychiatric care.

In the early months of 1994, we interviewed 223 victims of rape and sexual violence in 11 cities in Croatia, Slovenia, and Bosnia and Herzegovina. (We chose to interview in 11 cities in multiple countries in an attempt to reach a diverse group with different experiences.) We also interviewed other witnesses and victims of sexual violence, including

with volunteers who were not getting paid for their services. All this preparation, including securing funds for transportation costs and daily expenses such as food for the volunteers (which the United Nations would not allow me to pay for with money that I raised independently), took about six months.

men, in an effort to corroborate evidence and contextualise the sexual violence in the midst of the conflict. As a result, we collected detailed, concrete evidence of the systematic rape and sexual assault of women during the conflict and of the use of sexual violence as a tool of ethnic cleansing.

* * *

What we learned was beyond horrific, but summarising it briefly is important. We documented five 'patterns' of sexual violence and rape. The first was sexual violence in conjunction with looting and intimidation, which was present even before the full conflict erupted but increased as ethnic tensions grew. During these acts, paramilitary groups, gangs or individuals broke into people's homes, stole their belongings, attacked the residents and sexually assaulted the women, often in front of others. The second pattern we documented involved sexual violence committed during fighting, which involved armed forces attacking villages or towns, often times separating the area's people by age and sex. Then the forces would rape and sexually assault women, often in the women's homes, while they secured the area. Women sometimes were sexually assaulted publicly.

The third pattern we discovered was sexual violence at detention facilities. These sites, referred to as 'refugee collection centres', were used to house people who had been taken from their homes; upon arrival, individuals were separated by gender. Men of fighting age were often tortured, killed or forced into hard labor, while women were usually sent to different camps where they were held and then taken away to be raped and sexually assaulted by soldiers, paramilitaries, camp guards, and in some cases even civilians. After being raped or assaulted, the women were either brought back to the camps and killed there or held until they were released during prisoner exchanges. In these detention camps, which were basically used for mass executions, torture and other violations of humanitarian law, men were also subjected to rape and sexual violence.

The fourth pattern of rape and sexual violence we saw occurred at special camps that were used specifically for sexual violence. In these camps, women were routinely raped and abused, often subjected to torture and extreme violence that was regularly committed in front of other prisoners. These acts, as well as other less frequent occurrences, such as girls being forced to sit on landmines or jump out of windows, were done with the intent of humiliating those who were being held. We also learned that in some cases, women were raped at these camps to impregnate them and that they were held until their pregnancies were too far advanced for them to have abortions. The fifth and final pattern, which was related to the fourth, involved sexual violence in 'bordello' camps, places created specifically to hold women who could be raped and sexually assaulted by men returning from combat zones. These women were taken from their homes and camps, held in private houses or hotels, and forced to engage in sexual acts with men. The intent behind holding women in these 'bordellos' was not expressly to punish or harm them but to provide men with women they could rape and assault. And the women in these locations were usually killed, not released during prisoner exchanges.

* * *

Many of the women and young girls we interviewed were – not surprisingly – nervous and hesitant at the beginning of the process, but we were later told that many interviewees found their involvement in the investigation to be cathartic and even healing. The women who had been hurt so badly shared their stories, and word of our volunteers' careful and sensitive listening soon reached – and was respected by – others who had survived sexual violence and other injury in the conflict, including refugees. Because of this, the United Nations, some of whose bureaucrats put so many obstacles in the investigation's path, received positive recognition and appreciation from all around the world.

Despite the good reports and favourable reviews, however, the commission's work was terminated early in April 1994, and the rape and sexual violence investigation ended before we could interview a number of willing participants. By the end of March 1994, the commission was still receiving about 15 calls a day from people wanting to share their experiences.

* * *

Before we learned that the investigation would have to be cut short, we had hoped to expand our work in Bosnia and Herzegovina, the Federal Republic of Yugoslavia, and in other countries such as Turkey, where many refugees from the conflict were living. During the investigation, we frequently tried to interview rape and sexual violence victims in Serbia and Serb-held territories, but each time our requests were pushed off. In a final attempt to gain more data on rape and sexual violence victims in the Serb-dominated regions, I met with the Federal Republic of Yugoslavia's minister of justice in Geneva in March 1994, but we never received any data from the government.[23]

* * *

Torture and its putative justifications have persisted throughout history, and it is with a heavy heart that I see society continually overlook the lessons of the past. My own experiences in France and Egypt, which I think I never truly recovered from, were damaging, but I know I was spared the kind of torture and violations that I heard about in the former Yugoslavia. It's hard to describe the despair you feel sitting with someone who shows you his scars or a woman who describes her rape. Having seen its effects, I cannot countenance any arguments for the justification of torture. When basic human values are in the balance, torture cannot be tolerated, justified, rationalised or accepted. It is not sometimes acceptable. This is a line that cannot be partly crossed.

[23] A government report was submitted to another UN body in May 1994, which was an encouraging sign of some effort to preserve people's stories, but by then the commission had been terminated. We had no way to know whether the information in the government report was properly gathered, whether victims' identities were protected and whether those who were interviewed spoke freely.

March 1958: Cairo

AFTER SEVEN MONTHS of confinement, my first day out of my apartment was volatile. Haj Abdul Hamid and I walked leisurely, wondering whether we were being followed; sure enough, the two security men who had been posted at my building's entrance shadowed us so openly that passers-by could be forgiven for thinking that the men were our security detail. After a 20-minute walk we were heading home, hoping not to jeopardise the generosity the guards had offered the day before, when I ran into someone I knew from the neighbourhood. This was not surprising because I had lived there since 1947 except when I was at law school in France and Switzerland.

We stopped for the usual chatter, and when the neighbour asked the inevitable 'Where have you been for so long that I haven't see you in the neighborhood?', I gave a vague and hurried reply, eager to get away before he could catch onto my not-so-subtle security escorts. My hopes were too ambitious because as soon as the neighbour and I parted company, one of the security officers approached him and (as I found out later) asked what he and I had talked about.

Nothing more came of the chance encounter, but I had been warned. It was quite disappointing to realise that I could not interact with anyone without him or her being interrogated by the security detail and discovering that I was under the close watch of some intelligence agency. Despite the warning, however, I was impatient for the next day and spent all night envisioning what might happen. After setting aside other extravagant plans, I determined that I should go out alone, even though that would be difficult, since being alone filled me with fear. Was I going to be quietly picked up and disappear without anyone knowing my whereabouts? Would I be tortured? Fears dogged me, as did the image of the torture victim. Disappearances were numerous in Egypt in those days, and I was almost convinced that the security apparatus had planned an uneventful house confinement, knowing they would proceed to much more cruel actions. Would some staged accident leave me injured me or disabled? In my distraught state, the cautious move would have been to have Haj Abdul Hamid, who would be a witness and whose presence might keep the security officers from harming me, come along. But my mind was made up: this time, I would go alone.

* * *

As my left foot hit the pavement the next day, I thought about how symbolic this moment was for me. Under arrest with nothing ahead of me, I had sat on my fourth-floor balcony every day for hours and watched the people walk by. As the lives of others were parading before me, my own life was on hold.

I decided that I would embark alone at 8 am, the height of rush hour, when the presence of so many people increased the chance that that any foul play might be observed. I would give the security men no warning, no time to plan for how they might harm me. My tactical response to their holding me emotionally off-balance, always ill at ease, was to take them by surprise and do the unpredictable. (I had learned such tactics from my early passion for military history; I had read dozens of books about Napoleon and his campaigns, German General Erwin Rommel, and US generals George S. Patton and Douglas MacArthur.) I girded myself to go forward with audacity.

At exactly 8 am, I walked out of the building and nodded at the two security men, who were just arriving. They looked stupefied but nodded back, as if this was any normal interaction. I paused for a few seconds to give them a chance to recover. One of them reached for a walkie-talkie (while trying to conceal it). Then a 1957 black DeSoto sedan stopped and the rear window went down, revealing a big round face with thin hair and a strong neck on a big, heavy-set man. He was European and called to me by name. Although I barely recognised him, I went over to say hello.

Bruno Pinto stepped out of the car, greeted me effusively and asked about my mother, who had left Egypt for the United States a year earlier. Given that this man and his wife lived two blocks away, I surmised that my mother was the social connection. Pinto's father was the most prominent Italian doctor in Egypt, a man who directed one of the country's best hospitals, the Italian Hospital of Alexandria.

The Italian Hospital of Alexandria was established in the 1920s and employed Italian nuns as nurses and administrators. Although some physicians were Egyptians, the majority of the doctors working at the hospital were Italian. Bruno's brother, the family's business genius, led the Pinto Cotton Company, one of Egypt's largest cotton companies, which had ginning and spinning factories in Upper Egypt and exported cotton worldwide.

The Pinto family had also acquired a company that was one of the principal importers in Egypt at the time. The company, renamed the Franco-Pinto Import Company, was located in Cairo and led by Bruno. With 165 employees, it did an enormous volume of business that ranged in the millions back in the 1950s, which in those days was serious money, particularly in Egypt. The Franco-Pinto Import Company was Olivetti's agent for the Middle East and Africa. At the time, Olivetti, which manufactured typewriters and calculators, was among the technology giants, much like IBM, in the technological avant-garde.

Bruno and I chatted, exchanging generalities, and he reminded me about when we had first met, at one of my mother's famous parties. He said that the last thing he had heard about me was that I had gone to study abroad, and now here I was back in Cairo. He then asked what I did for a living. I paused, not knowing what to say. In addition to being under house arrest, I had no job and no passport that would have allowed me to leave the country. I knew, however, that this was not a subject I could discuss with him. As I struggled to come up with a response, I could feel four sets of eyes behind me trained on us, trying to determine what we were going on about in Italian. One of the security officers following me was already on his walkie-talkie, and I could only imagine his news moving quickly up the chain of command: 'Suspect speaks in a foreign language to a strange-looking European who came for him at 0800, and security had no prior notice of the meeting.' I could not imagine what sorts of agitated questions this must have triggered.

I could tell that my vague responses disturbed Bruno; I imagine he must have thought I had turned into a bourgeois playboy who could live comfortably off his parents' wealth. He kept nudging me about working, and he presented all sorts of arguments for why I should put my talents to use. I, of course, agreed without dispute. I think he might have thought I wanted to work but did not know how to go about it or maybe was embarrassed to ask. Why not work for him in his import business?

'After all', he said, 'you speak six languages, have travelled the world with your parents and studied abroad, and your family's connections would be a great asset.'

What could I say? I gave an inane answer, something to the effect of 'Let me think about it.'

He spoke quickly. At 8 am the following morning, he said, he would come pick me up and take me to the office. We would spend the day there, and then at 3 pm I would join him for lunch at his house.

Before I could answer, he patted me on the back, shook my hand, returned to his car and departed. This could be a real turning point in my life, I thought. But how could I get around the fact that I was prohibited from working? And for a foreign company, to boot? I stood on the sidewalk, with two curious security officers behind me, trying to figure out what to do. When I saw one of the security officers again on his walkie-talkie, I informed him loudly that Bruno Pinto, a social acquaintance of my mother, had invited me to visit his office the next day, and if there were any reservations, he should please notify me. None was expressed. Haj Abdul Hamid did not come that afternoon, so I was not able to get his advice. After an almost sleepless night, I decided to chance the next day's programme, and if Bruno offered me a job, I would find a reason to refuse.

***

I was awake and ready to go long before 8 am the next morning, at my front door two minutes before Bruno was to pick me up. When a black police car with a driver and two security officers arrived, I walked over to the car and (to the officers' astonishment) politely said 'good morning' and announced that I was spending the day at Pinto's office and then lunching at his home. I gave them both addresses. The officer, apparently impressed with my openness, thanked me.

In the black DeSoto I sat in the back next to Bruno, who was already smoking a pipe (which I took to be auspicious, given my own pipe-smoking habit since Dijon). Bruno told me that Franco-Pinto Import Company represented Dunhill in Egypt, that they were the world's finest pipe-makers whose pipes were as beautiful as their prices. When we arrived at the office, Bruno gave me a sample from Dunhill's new pipe line, which I happily accepted. By my standards it would have cost a fortune, but he had gotten it for free. He smoked it to test the product before merchandising it, he said. Would I be willing to accept it for the same purpose? I did, of course. I kept the pipe for decades, even after I quit smoking. It has been part of my history, a token of renewed hope in my bleakest hours.

That first day Bruno had me sit in on all his briefings, even private meetings with his senior management. I did not make a peep; I listened attentively and apparently answered Bruno's questions with some degree of intelligence and good sense. He was pleased and I tried to give the impression that I was in control, but I was still bewildered about how and when to tell him about my house arrest and the apparent prohibition on my working.

At lunch at Bruno's home, I charmed his wife with well-worn stories. After the meal, we smoked our pipes, and as we puffed away he offered me a position as his personal assistant. I would work with him, travel with him, and in about a year I would be poised for a junior-management position, but the path to advancement would be fast. I absorbed every word as if it were a balm to my wounded soul. With such a job, I could finish my legal education at the University of Cairo law school, launch a business career, stay away from the military and the government, and continue to manage my family's farmlands.

But how should I handle the security problem? My mind raced, and I came up with a plan: I would accept Bruno's proposal but ask to take a week to ten days before starting the job and then move heaven and earth with relatives and friends to nudge security into allowing me to work while avoiding involving Bruno and his family in my issues with the GIA.

Bruno agreed to the ten-day postponement, though he did insist I return to the office the next day to go over some administrative matters. I guessed he wanted to formalise our deal so that I would not back out of it. When he picked me up at 8 am the next morning, the same black security car with the same officers followed us to his office. There we had coffee and sat through morning briefings (at which I was introduced as his personal assistant). By mid-morning, I was completing paperwork in the personnel office.

When I was summoned to Pinto's office two hours later, I froze. From the frown on Pinto's face, I could tell that the security officers had come to inquire about me. They had questioned Pinto for about an hour. How did he know me? What did he want with me? And much more. They concluded by informing him that I could not work because I was under investigation as a possible security threat to the Egyptian state, telling Bruno only that they represented the GIA. After Bruno asked them, innocently, for something in writing so he could officially terminate me, the men replied that the GIA did not work that way and that if he knew what was best for him, his family and their business interests, he would just cooperate. The officers certainly rubbed Bruno, a successful businessman who had had no dealings with abusive security people, the wrong way.

Now, in his office, it was my turn to answer questions. What did I have to do with the GIA? Nothing, I said, other than intercessions on behalf of two Jewish families. Was that all? He pressed me repeatedly, and I repeatedly said that was all. And I explained what had happened.

December 1956: Cairo

IT HAD STARTED a few months earlier, in December 1956, well before
my house arrest and even before my return to France, during the
period when the Nasser regime ordered the expulsion of French and
British nationals as well as Egyptian Jews. The Nasser regime – and
many Egyptians – were anti-Jewish because of Israel's attack on Egypt
in concert with the British and French. Many Jews had foreseen these
negative consequences when the state of Israel had been established in
1948, but the situation unspooled for them in Egypt only after the 1956
Suez War.

The 1956 wave of expulsions included families that had been in Egypt
for generations. With the Egyptian Army's defeat in the Sinai Desert still
fresh in people's minds, there was little hope for due process in deciding
who would be expelled. Those in the regime who executed this policy
profited from the distress of others by buying the property, furniture
and cars left behind at very low prices. Expulsion orders were frequently
executed within a week – nowhere near enough time for anyone to settle
affairs.

On 7 November 1956, the 1956 war officially ended with the implementation of UN General Assembly resolution 997. In early December,
I was still in uniform and stationed at Marouf military training camp
in West Cairo on that seemingly uneventful day when my father asked
me go on his behalf to Café El Shams, on 26 July Street, opposite the
Supreme Court building, to ask whether anyone had found a leather
cigar holder he had left there the night before. Although he lived in Alexandria, whenever he was in Cairo he frequented this café in the evenings
and met his retiree friends there. Such cafés were – and continue to be –
the main social gathering points for Egyptians from all walks of life.
People converse across the tables, over the ashtrays and coffee cups;
strangers frequently pull up a chair and join a circle in the open arena
of social discourse. Although people maintain class distinctions, making
their social standing apparent in where they sit and whom they talk to,
in the cafés both rich and poor assemble.

On my way to the café, which was within walking distance of my
camp, I bumped into someone hunched over and sobbing in the crowded
street. It was Professor Haroun Haddad, my old teacher from my Jesuit

high school. He told me he had just received a notice of expulsion giving him one week to leave the country. He had gone to the police to prove that his family had been born, had lived and had been buried in Egypt for 300 years – to no avail.

I had not realised that the expulsion orders applied to anyone other than British and French nationals, and I had no idea Professor Haddad was Jewish. The authorities, he said, had told him he needed some other proof of citizenship such as a passport or military discharge papers, but because he had never travelled abroad or served in the military, he had neither. He had only his birth certificate and evidence that his ancestors were buried in a local graveyard. But that was not enough.

Outraged, I walked with him to his apartment, where he and his wife were in great distress. After drinking the obligatory tea offered by Mrs Haddad, I proceeded to the headquarters of the GIA, which was several blocks from where I was living in Garden City. The building, off Kasr El Ainy Street, was nondescript, but most people in Cairo crossed the street in fear, just to avoid walking past it. I doubt that anyone in recent years, certainly no one of my modest age and lowly rank who had no official business, ever dared barge into the building as I did.

But in my mind, I was the third generation of Bassiounis to fight for Egypt's freedom, in uniform and the equivalent of a second lieutenant in the National Guard. My father was a retired ambassador. My grandfather had been the president of the Senate, a historic figure and national hero. My second cousin was a major-general and commander of the Artillery Corps. Other relatives included a lieutenant-general, the head of the Corps of Engineers, and a retired army lieutenant-colonel. My family's long history in Egypt's service, in addition to my own brief military career, armed me with immense pluck – or perhaps clouded my judgement.

And so I made my way to the director's office, past various officials who demanded to know whether I had an appointment, whether the director was expecting me, or whether I was a relative or friend. They probably thought I was cracked. After a brief skirmish involving armed men, shouts, screams and orders to put my hands up, everyone suddenly saluted someone who had just entered the lobby, surrounded by others. At the centre of the group was a distinguished-looking man with a thin Clark Gable mustache dressed in a charcoal-grey suit with a silk burgundy moiré tie. (The tie was the hallmark of a renowned Paris haberdasher by the name of Sulka. President Nasser wore Sulka ties, and those in the highest-ranking positions, both government and private, copied him.) He was Ali Sabri, the director of the agency.

Sabri was a member of the former Revolutionary Command Council; his rank at the time of the revolution was Air Force wing commander. He directed the GIA from 1954 to 1957 and then became head of a governmental holding company that controlled all government-held companies, beginning with the 1957 wave of nationalisations of private-sector industry and culminating with a new wave of nationalisation after 1967.

The director and his guards, perhaps thinking that I posed no threat, eventually said I could see him. It was like 'open sesame': I was given a badge proclaiming 'Visitor' by the man at the reception desk. Two of the armed security guards were at my sides, their guns now in their holsters. To everyone's obvious dismay, I was escorted to the main lift. The lift stopped at the seventh floor, where there was a large reception area with more guards. I was taken to a waiting room and offered coffee or tea. An officer from the director's entourage sat with me in the reception room, carefully observing me.

Was I nervous? he asked.

I said of course I was nervous. But my message was important.

'Important for whom? And why?'

My response, wholly spontaneous, was, 'Important for the integrity of the revolution.'

In his office, the director asked my name and rank, and after consulting a thin file, confirmed my family connections (yes, my father was former ambassador Ibrahim Bassiouni; yes, my grandfather was Senator Mahmoud Bassiouni; and yes, Ali Bassiouni, a retired lieutenant-colonel from the Army Supply Corps, was my father's brother, my uncle). We exchanged stories confirming that Ali Bassiouni had never really been suited to the military (he brought in a lector to read from the Qur'an, for instance, assembled poor people in his office to whom he gave charity, and greeted news of the theft of 1,000 blankets by warehouse personnel with an offer to pay for them). We also talked a little about my second cousin, Major-General Abdel Moneim Riad.

I proceeded at last to tell him of Professor Haddad and concluded by saying that for the integrity of the revolution, all Egyptians – and for that matter, all non-Egyptians – had to be treated with respect. It was unconscionable to have Egyptians expelled from their country of birth. He listened carefully, his eyes burrowing into me. I thought I saw an attempt to find what motivated my protestations and what my intentions were. I think my sincerity came through. He wrote down some of the information, told me he would look into it and proceeded to dismiss me in the same superior military tone he had used when I first came in. I stood at attention, did a military about-face and walked out of the office in the proper military stride.

The two armed guards returned me to the lift and then down to the reception hall, where I returned my badge to the bewildered receptionist. The moment I stepped out of the building, I exhaled a sigh of relief so large that it could have been heard a block away. As I walked to my apartment in Garden City, I kept thanking God for the fortuitous arrival of director Sabri when I was about to be arrested.

I called Professor Haddad, who was astounded, to tell him what I had done. He and his wife, who passed the phone between them, were so profuse in their gratitude that I felt rewarded for any risks I might have taken.

In the afterglow of this incident, I could not help telling anyone who wanted to listen about my march into the GIA building on someone else's behalf. Three days later, however, Professor Haddad called and told me dejectedly that the order of expulsion had not been revoked but he had been given an extra thirty days to produce documents of his Egyptian citizenship. In the end, he was not able to satisfy the police officer in charge of his file, but my ego made me oblivious to both the gravity and the callous unfairness of the situation.

Two weeks after the Haddad episode, my mother called me at the military camp in downtown Cairo. She told me that one of the friends she played bridge with, a French-born widow of a prominent Egyptian personality with a daughter about my age, had been asked to leave the country. I remembered my mother's friend well, particularly because I had a strong infatuation with her daughter, who, I thought, was one of the most beautiful women I had ever seen; I would have climbed Mount Everest to get to know her. But we were both about 18 years old at the time we met, and a girl of 18 does not look with much interest at boys her age.

I was probably too immature at the time to impress her, so she remained something of a distant vision in my mind until the day my mother called to tell me about the family's plight. They had only a week to leave Egypt, my mother explained, because they were French dual citizens and also Jewish. She said that the police officer who delivered the expulsion order had been rudely flirtatious with the daughter.

My male ego kicked in, and I asked my commanding officer for special permission to leave camp for two hours on an urgent matter. In the GIA building, I was relieved to see the same person on duty in the reception booth. He acknowledged me with a smile and this time, upon hearing that I wanted to see the director but had no appointment, did not call the guards but telephoned the director's office. Once again, I went to the seventh-floor waiting room, received tea and waited until I was ushered into the director's office. I began the meeting by thanking him for what he had done for Professor Haddad (which I came to learn later was all he expected: a strictly formal and brief thank you and a goodbye). But then I told him about my mother's friend and her daughter, making sure to describe the police officer's inappropriate behaviour toward the daughter. That last part did not sit well with him, and I saw a frown cross his face. He called someone from his secretariat and asked him to take the information from me and told me that I was dismissed. In a threatening way, he added, 'Do not ever come back here again.'

I quickly did a formal about-face, left the office, gave my information to the director's staff and left the building. To my surprise, my mother's friend called her the next day to thank her. Like Professor Haddad, she still had to leave Egypt but had been given a ten-day extension, which gave her a little extra time to get her affairs in order. She added that the policeman who came to see her had apologised for the earlier captain's improper behaviour.

* * *

When I related all this to Bruno Pinto, he paused and asked me one question.

'Would you do it again?'

Without hesitation, I answered, 'For friends and family, yes.'

Bruno nodded, puffing on his pipe, with a look of tranquility I could not decipher. As if to change the subject, he asked about my house arrest, and I described my reaction to the photograph of the torture victim and my threat to publicly denounce the agencies who did such things because I was convinced that President Nasser could not possibly be aware of these terrible practices – or if he was aware, not stop them.

'Were you serious?', Bruno asked.

Again, without hesitation, I said yes, asking how I could possibly face God if I had seen what was happening and done nothing.

What would I have done if I had been in Germany during the Second World War, he asked. I said I would have killed 'Uncle Hitler' and told him about running with my toy gun, at four years old, into the siren-filled street.

Bruno Pinto looked at me quizzically, "You are very different."

I corrected him; I was really just doing the right thing, what most people should be doing.

Pinto's response brought tears to my eye: 'As long as I am the head of this company', he said, 'you will have a job here.' From that moment on, he had my gratitude and loyalty.

I did not know then that the Pintos were an old Sephardic Jewish family and that in 1948, after the establishment of the state of Israel, all the Egyptian Pintos had converted to Catholicism. Socially they were known as Catholics with no connection to Judaism, even less so to Israel, but that was not what the GIA knew or believed, and I cannot guess what Bruno was thinking as he listened to my story of interceding on behalf of Professor Haddad and my mother's friend and her daughter.

When I began working for the Pintos, I did not know that the GIA was continuing to compile the ever-growing file it had on me. I also had no notion that, in the eyes of the GIA, my time working for the Pintos shifted my designation from someone who had simply interceded on behalf of close Jewish friends to a 'Jewish sympathizer'. I did not learn any of this for some time, until my second cousin, Major-General Abdel Moneim Riad, enlightened me.

April 2011: Various Locations in Libya

I WONDER IF perhaps I have been constantly improvising these many decades, happening on ways out of tight corners. But with improvisation comes risk.

In Libya in April 2011, I received an email from a former student, Kristen Frost, telling me that a friend of a friend who was working as a freelance journalist in Libya had been kidnapped and detained by forces loyal to Muammar el-Qaddafi. The journalist's name was James Foley. This was the first time I had heard of an American being held by the Qaddafi regime. I added his name to my list of journalists detained by Qaddafi's forces, including those I had met during my investigation, a total of 27, and decided to do my best secure his release when I arrived in Tripoli a few days later.

Even as chair of the UN Commission of Inquiry, I could not enter Tripoli because NATO was bombing it. Determined to fulfil the Commission of Inquiry's mandate, I called the secretary-general of NATO and asked his help getting in. It took some negotiation, but he finally told me to go to Malta and contact a specific charter company. NATO, he said, would suspend bombing for 48 hours to allow me to get into Tripoli. I chartered a plane from Malta and made the trip, accompanied by two commission colleagues and a number of staff members.

Upon arrival, I tried to meet with Abdel Rahman Shalgham, a former foreign minister whom I had met when he was Libya's ambassador to Italy. But Shalgham could not make it into the city and delegated the secretary-general of Qaddafi's party, Mohammad Abu al-Qasim al-Zwai, to meet with us. With him were the attorney general, the minister of justice, and the deputy minister of foreign affairs, Mohamed Abdul Aziz, whom I had met before. When I told them that I wanted the Commission of Inquiry's delegation to criss-cross part of Libya over the next 48 hours to observe some of the towns where fighting had taken place, the secretary-general asked with a half-smirk, 'Why don't you stay here indefinitely? That way NATO will stop bombarding us.'

I responded with something to the effect of, 'Well, it would cost you.'

'We'll pay anything', he replied.

I presented him with the list of the 27 journalists, which he looked at blankly and then passed to his colleagues. 'If we can find them', he said, 'we'll release them.'

I started telling him the locations of those I knew: James Foley and a Canadian journalist of Arab origin who had been imprisoned and whom Canada wanted back. He told me that these things were possible.[24]

I told him I wanted something else, however, and went on to discuss the case of Iman al-Obeidi, who had been interviewed by commission members. Al-Obeidi, a Libyan postgraduate law student, had appeared at a hotel in Tripoli in late March 2011 and told members of the international press corps there that she had been beaten and gang-raped by Libyan troops. Her public statement – and the worldwide attention it received – challenged both the Qaddafi government and the taboo against discussing sex crimes. I said I believed she was still being held, and I wanted her to be allowed to leave the country. I told them I understood that Tunisia was willing to take her.

Again, they told me that would be fine. I said I wanted to speak with her then to verify that she was still alive but received only a phone number, which I was able to call the next day to tell her of her impending release. She was released to Tunis within the 48 hours. I have not communicated with her since, but she will always remain part of my life's story – and I a character in hers.

All 27 journalists were also released. While I was in Tripoli for those 48 hours, I went to see the Canadian journalist in prison and told him he was going to be released. He had tears in his eyes.

---

[24] Foley's capture in Libya did not dim his passion for telling stories of life in warzones. He was back in Libya by October where he was present for the capture and death of el-Qaddafi. Sadly, however, after leaving Libya Foley was captured in Syria on 22 November, 2012, by militia forces loyal to the Syrian government of President Bashar al-Assad. He remained detained until video of his death at the hands of ISIS was posted on the internet on 19 August, 2014.

April 1993: The Former Yugoslavia

DURING OUR FIRST initial field investigation in the former Yugoslavia, I quickly learned that no one was immune from the tremendous divide, in communities small and large, that was the cause of the ongoing conflict – not even those whose job was to preach of love and forgiveness.

In the days before we arrived in Sarajevo, some of the commission members and I had many meetings in Belgrade. At one, I met with His Holiness Pope Pavle, the 83-year-old leader of the Serbian Orthodox Church, who revealed to me his deep dismay over the ongoing violence in the region, particularly in Bosnia-Herzegovina. While I sensed his that concerns were genuine and that he really would have liked to help restore peace to the region, others told me that he was surrounded by many militant nationalist clerics in the Synod who were less ready to speak out against Serbian violence. His Holiness told me that he had had a private, unpublicised meeting with the Roman Catholic archbishop of Zagreb only a few weeks before we arrived and that the two men wanted to find a way to issue a joint appeal to reduce the violence. I encouraged him to include the senior imam of Sarajevo, Moustofa Ceirc, in this effort. His Holiness indicted he would like to do so but for political reasons could not.

While I understood that this man's role as a religious leader in the midst of an ethnically and religiously charged conflict made him a de facto political leader, I privately struggled with his failure to speak out. Because I firmly believe in the power of shared values of the world's religions, I was truly bothered that once again, the commonality of the Abrahamic religions and the shared humanity among all people were not enough to overcome politics and violence. But this was far from the greatest frustration of the commission members' 34 on-site field investigations.

1960s and 1970s: Cairo

IN 1957, WHEN I was under house arrest, my second cousin, Major-General Abdel Moneim Riad, then chief of staff of Egypt's artillery, went to see Salah Nasr, the head of the GIA, to speak on my behalf.

During Nasr's tenure, more people were arrested as political prisoners and tortured by GIA or police state security forces than ever before: communists, Muslim Brotherhood members, old regime supporters, opponents of any kind, even if they did nothing but voice their opposition to the Nasser regime and its practices.

As he later told me, Major-General Riad knew that when Nasr had transferred to the GIA from the army three years before, he had been only a major, and when he sat across from Nasr that day, my cousin was facing a man who, to him, was still a major. So he considered it a serious breach of military protocol that Nasr didn't even have the courtesy to come out from behind his desk and sit next to him.

As my cousin later told me, he took off his military cap, placed it in on the table before him, and told Nasr, 'I came here to talk to you about my relative Cherif Bassiouni.'

Nasr, Major-General Riad said, pushed a button and summoned someone to find and deliver my file, which happened within minutes. At Nasr's order, the plainclothes officer summarised the case: Mahmoud Cherif Bassiouni, son of El-Sayed Ibrahim Bassiouni, grandson of Mahmoud Ibrahim Bassiouni, had three files: the first for being a Jewish sympathizer, the second for being a Muslim Brotherhood sympathizer, and the third for belonging to a prominent family of the old regime.

Major-General Riad said he asked the officer how someone could possibly be a Jewish sympathiser (who presumably supported the state of Israel), a veteran decorated for military valour (who had fought against British and French forces, which were allied with Israel) at Port Said, and a sympathiser of the Muslim Brotherhood (which everyone knew was unsympathetic to Jews and Israel). And how could such a person be anti-regime, even if he came from a prominent family, when his grandfather had led Egypt's 1919 revolution against the British, had been imprisoned and sentenced to death by them, and later had become Egypt's first president of the Senate?

The plainclothes officer said, 'This is a complicated case', and Nasr dismissed him. At this point, my cousin told me, he was expecting some answers from Nasr and was flabbergasted to hear Nasr say, 'General Riad, with all due respect, I suggest you forget about this matter and never talk about it again', a statement he considered grossly impertinent, especially coming from a mid-level officer.

'I am sorry, Cherif', my second cousin said years later, 'but I picked up my cap, put it on my head, said goodbye without even looking at Nasr or shaking hands with him, and left the room.'

* * *

After my release from house arrest, although my circumstances were becoming more tolerable, I was sure that even if I did not encounter GIA officers for years, if they wanted to find me anytime anywhere in the world, they could. I never understood why I was the subject of so much animosity and suspicion from the regime, and my nerves never completely relaxed until 1974, when President Anwar el-Sadat personally ordered my GIA files destroyed. Even so, I suspect that a summary, with my name on it, survives somewhere in some bigger file. Intelligence agencies' memories are always long.

March 1958–December 1961: Cairo and Alexandria

AFTER BRUNO PINTO was kind enough to disregard the GIA's warnings about my working for his import company, I threw myself into the job, eager to learn anything and everything I could. Around the second week of March 1958, I realised that I had either been released from house arrest or the surveillance had been greatly reduced: the security officers were no longer stationed just beyond my doorstep, and I was not followed to and from work. I still did not have my passport, however, so for all intents and purposes I was trapped in Egypt.

After spring became summer and summer became autumn, Bruno informed me that he and his family were going to Italy for their annual family holiday. When he told me in late September that they had decided to extend their stay, I thought nothing of it and said I would see him when he returned.

Then in October, a member of the chief prosecutor's office in Cairo arrived at the company's office with a contingent of police officers and soldiers and informed a hastily assembled group that the government had ordered the Pinto companies seized on the basis that the owners were Jewish, that they had fled the country, and that they had illegally removed assets.

When the office manager protested that the Pintos were Catholics, the prosecutor said they had converted to Catholicism only to protect themselves and their assets in Egypt. It suddenly occurred to me why Bruno Pinto had given me a job despite the GIA's surveillance and dire warnings – and what had been behind our conversation that day in his office: I had stood up for Jews. He was a Jew, and he had stood up for me when I was in need.

Two days later an Austrian gentleman, Willie Hendrix, arrived and met with the top managers of the Pinto companies (which, to my amazement, included me), saying he was a Pinto family friend who had come to Egypt to keep as many company and family assets as he could out of government hands. When he asked for someone to serve as executor and represent the Pinto family's interests, I knew the time had come for me to show my gratitude to Bruno Pinto. All the Pinto companies' stock was soon put in my name. The Pintos held multiple companies, some of them led by a chairman of the board and president and all of them with a general manager, as required by Egyptian corporate law. As the new owner, I appointed myself to all these positions, unaware that when the government completed its seizure of the Pinto assets and nationalised their companies, I would still be legally considered the senior administrator of all the companies.

Over the next few months, Willie Hendrix and I combined all the Pintos' companies into the United Arab Company for Commerce and Industry (UACCI), and I did what I could to protect these assets from seizure and block a judicial finding that the Pintos had illegally taken assets out of the country, which could have led to their extradition from Italy and prosecution in Egypt. This potential prosecution of the Pintos turned into the seed of my interest in extradition law.

A final judicial decree eventually declared that the government had seized and nationalised the Pintos' former companies, but fortunately, by that time a former government attorney had taken over as the chairman and president of the newly conglomerated UACCI. I remained as general manager but was eventually transferred by the Mu'asassa al-Iqtisadiām or Economic Institution, the government agency responsible for nationalised private-sector entities, to its central offices, which oversaw the government's newly acquired assets, including those of the British, French and Jews who had been expelled and Egyptians whose property had been seized because they were 'anti-regime'.

The head of that agency turned out to be Ali Sabri, the man whom I had visited twice when he was the director of the GIA, but because I was only a small cog in an enormous bureaucratic machine, I'm pleased to say that he never knew I was on his agency's staff.

What a funny turn of fate: after months of house arrest for being an anti-government agitator, I had a new career as a government employee, accorded the rank of a former general manager of a now-nationalised company, with an official title and salary. And this new position would finally get me out from under the government's thumb.

April 1958–December 1961: Cairo

BECAUSE OF MY arrest in France, short stint in Geneva and subsequent house arrest in Egypt, I had not been able to finish my law degree, so while working for the Pinto companies from 1958 to 1961, I registered for classes at the University of Cairo's law school. My work made attending classes difficult, but I managed to make it to my final year, although I left Egypt six months before my graduation. Nevertheless, years later I was granted the equivalent of a bachelor of law degree from the University of Cairo.

One day, a few months after I was officially released from my unofficial house arrest, I was invited to the US embassy to a talk given by Thomas Sorenson, then information officer and press attaché at the US embassy in Beirut, who later advised President John F. Kennedy (for whom his brother, Ted Sorenson, wrote speeches) on foreign affairs. He was introduced by the director of the local office of the US Information Agency (USIA), a striking young woman whom I thought much too young to hold such an important position, particularly because she was Egyptian and such posts were usually reserved for US diplomats. But she had graduated at the top of her class at the American University in Cairo and had then become the assistant to the president of the university. When the university president subsequently became the US ambassador, he had the State Department hire her at the USIA. She was tasked with the job of bringing in speakers from the United States and exposing Egyptian intelligentsia and officials to American thinking. Her name was Adele, she was a Copt, a member of the largest Christian denomination in Egypt, and she was five years older than me.

Adele organised USIA events with a poise and thoughtfulness that came through her deep voice when she spoke. I was fascinated by her, but it was only after a second meeting at the USIA that I dared approach her and ask, in a very clumsy way, whether she would accept my invitation to have dinner. Her answer took me off guard; she said she knew everything that needed to be known about me and my family, and instead of accepting my invitation, she invited me to accompany her to a dinner reception given by the US ambassador. That same evening I picked her up at her home and saw her for the first time in more modern dress. I was captivated. She must have noticed because she smiled a lot during the drive from her home to the ambassador's residence, and she frequently reminded me to pay attention to the road. The entire evening I could not take my eyes off her, which apparently was obvious enough that at one point an American journalist approached me and said something to the effect of 'you look quite taken with your date'.

Ours was a challenging match. Coptic–Muslim personal relations have always been difficult in Egypt, and at the time intermarriage was rare. Our age difference, not necessarily a barrier for people much older, was significant for a 20-year-old and 25-year-old. Even though I did not look much younger than she did, the disparity was evident. Although I had faced tests that many mature men could not even conceive of, my social development had not progressed much beyond my family and college experiences. Perhaps most important, though I didn't know it at the time, after so long under house arrest, I was experiencing post-traumatic stress. Adele, whom I nicknamed Addy, became my de facto psychologist.

Our temperaments were radically different. She was calm, reserved and able to be cautious in all she said. I was the exact opposite. But for some reason, we were a good match; to me she was a psychological anchor, and I think to her I was a challenge. Given that we came from the same conservative Egyptian milieu, which did not really differ much for Muslims, Christians and Jews, each of us expected we would respect the other, our faiths and our customs.

We became very attached. Several months into our relationship, I proposed marriage; she said that while she wanted it, her family would never approve, and she would be ostracised. This struck me as a sort of classical Greek tragedy in which love and duty are at odds: our archetypal conflict centred on a Christian marrying a Muslim in Egypt. We both promised to try to find a way forward together, and less than a month later she came up with a scheme in which she could get a job at the USIA in Washington, I could find work or continue my education there, and then we could reopen the subject of marriage.

I said I was ready to go anytime she was. We carried on, fantasising about how our future would unfold. We were very much in love, and together we dreamed of the day when we could put our plan into action, begin new lives in the United States, and be married.

* * *

During this time, a time when Egypt was forcing its citizens to leave, a time when I was fearful that at any moment I would be placed back under house arrest, tortured or even worse, I learned that my mother had been diagnosed with cancer. She had left Egypt the year before, in 1957, and was living with her new husband, an American named Howard Hutchens, in Indianapolis. When I learned of her illness, I knew that I needed to leave Egypt to be with her, no matter what the obstacles.

My first approach was to leave legally, and I requested through the proper administrative channels that my passport, which had been seized in August 1957 when I was placed on house arrest, be reinstated so I could leave the country to visit my mother. My request (not surprisingly, given the Egyptian intelligence community's opinions of me) was denied. But I was determined to be with my mother, so I needed another plan.

Under the tight dictatorship of the Nasser regime, this was going to be a huge challenge. With no passport and no exit visa, I could not buy a plane or boat ticket to leave Egypt and, obviously, could not legally enter another country. Airports and port facilities were high-security zones, closely guarded, with no easy entrance. By land, there were three possible exits: Israel to the east, Libya to the west, and Sudan to the south. But all three borders were heavily patrolled, and there was no way to sneak across them.

Ironically, or perhaps fatefully, my work as a government official required me to go inside the port area in Alexandria, for which I had a special permit, quite frequently. During my visits to the customs port area, I had noticed a security gap. Probably because security was so strict outside the customs area, inside that perimeter, in the place where passengers were checked before boarding ships, including cruise ships, security was lax. This, I decided, was my best route out.

But the problem of getting a passport and exit visa remained, and I knew that without them I could not buy a boat ticket. (Getting a visa for Italy, where my mother and I had decided to meet, and getting onto the boat to Italy undetected were issues I decided to worry about later.) I was still plagued with fear that if I were caught trying to sneak out of Egypt, I would be killed or spend years in prison and be tortured there. But I also I reminded myself that my mother needed me.

In devising my plan, I decided to rely on the Egyptian bureaucracy's mindless processes, and I officially applied for a new passport. The worst that could happen, I decided, was that my application would be denied, and I would be in the same position I was already in.

A few days after submitting my application, I went to the passport office late in the day, around 3 pm, when all the duty officers seemed to have left for the day. Only a warrant officer and a few sergeants and soldiers remained, so I approached the warrant officer, gave him my name and asked if my passport had been issued. To my surprise and delight, he located my passport, which had been issued but had not been stamped or signed by the officer in charge. I asked the warrant officer if he would stamp the passport for me so that when the officer in charge came, he could just sign it. Accepting a little *baksheesh* (bribe), from me, he said, 'I'll take care of it.' The officer took my passport into a back room for a bit while I waited nervously and soon returned, saying he had stamped the passport but the officer in charge had not been able to sign it because he was too busy. I could, he suggested, leave the passport there and come back the next day to pick it up, after it had been signed. I told him I would just take the passport and bring it back for the signature, and I left, knowing I would not dare return.

On my way out, I asked one of the many people leaving with passports if I could inspect his; the stamp on his completed passport, I saw, was identical to mine, missing only the scribbled signature of the officer in charge. I decided to risk using the stamped passport with no signature, hoping no one would notice. (The lawyer in me, concerned about a charge of forgery, prevented me from adding a little scribbled signature to the stamp.)

The next day I visited the Italian consulate, and because of my connection to the Pintos, the vice-consul immediately issued me a three-month tourist visa. Then, with my new passport and new visa, I bought a ticket on a luxury liner from Alexandria to Genoa. Luckily for me, the travel agent did not notice that I had no exit visa and sold me the ticket. A few days later I would be on the Italian liner, the *Esperia*, heading to Italy. But first I needed to board the boat without getting caught.

December 1961: Alexandria, Aboard the Esperia

I T WAS ON 9 December 1961, my 24th birthday, that I escaped – a fact that was not lost on me as I prepared to leave my home country under very contentious circumstances. I had my passport and my ticket; all I needed to do was board the ship without detection and remain undetected by Egyptian authorities until we had reached international waters. I made my way to the customs area of the port of Alexandria in the late afternoon the day before departure, using the special permit I had from work. I hid there until 2 am and then, along with other passengers eager to be ready for the early-morning departure, boarded the ship. I used the darkness of night as my cover, and no one saw me.

April 2011: Libya

MANY DECADES LATER, I undertook another boarder crossing, equally fraught with obstacles, administrative and otherwise, but for very different reasons.

I had been appointed chairman of a commission of inquiry into the allegations of human rights violations in Libya, and, as in the former Yugoslavia, I was determined to see for myself what was unfolding on the ground.

As we were planning our trip and investigations, the conflict ravaging the country was beginning to intensify. We needed to go into the field to investigate, but we needed approval from the people in New York who were in charge of security. They were in New York, but they got to decide what could happen in Libya.

'You can't go to Libya', they said.

But by then, on my fifth international investigation, I understood the tricks of the game.

'Can I go to Cairo?', I asked.

'Oh, of course you can go to Cairo', they said.

So I went to Cairo, which for the second time in my life became my springboard.

In Cairo I asked, 'Can I go to the border?'

The authorities said, 'Oh, sure, you can go to Siwa', which is about 550 km from Cairo, very close to the Libyan border.

And I said, 'Can I get into Libya?'

Oh, no, they said. To do that I needed armour-plated cars, and I didn't have armour-plated cars. That, of course, was just an excuse. (You have to think in these bureaucratic terms.)

So I called some people that I knew in the Egyptian military, and they got the military at the border to cooperate with me. At the border, every time I saw a UN car, either a car from the UN High Commissioner for Refugees or from UNICEF, we would stop it. I would talk to the driver and the person being transported, and I would ask, 'Who is your boss?' Then I would call the boss in Cairo and ask if I could have the car.

And the boss would say, 'Well, of course you can't have my car.'

And I would say, 'Relax. I have a car like it in Cairo. I will give it to you in trade, but I need this car because it supposedly has armour plates on it that will save us.' And so, after a little bit of back and forth, I was able to trade five cars.

I had a team of 25 people, so we decided that we would skip the driver and have one of our security personnel take the wheel. To make sure we could proceed unharmed, I used my Egyptian contacts to call people in Benghazi, and they sent a couple of people to guide us through.

The problem was, we had not anticipated the strong easterly winds that prevail in March and April, winds of 60–80 km per hour that blow a lot of sand in the desert and make driving extremely difficult. We drove about 2,000 km – 1,000 kilometers there and 1,000 back, not knowing where to stop. We stopped at whatever big building we thought was a hotel. Sometimes somebody was in it; sometimes it was empty. We had trouble finding food and water, but we proceeded and kept at our task. Our job was full of improvisation.

December 1961: Aboard the Esperia, Genoa, Milan, Vienna

ONCE ABOARD THE ship, I hid inside a lifeboat on the uppermost deck until about 2 pm the next day, until the boat had reached international waters. Breathing a sigh of relief, I went and found the ship's purser to ask for my cabin. I was on the passenger list and I had a first-class ticket, a passport and a visa to Italy, so everything was in order. But the purser, suspicious about why someone would take more than 24 hours to ask for his cabin, took me to the captain. I told the captain that I had been so exhausted when I boarded the ship that I simply fell asleep on one of the chaise longues on the upper deck and had just awakened. The captain said he had never heard of someone sleeping so long, but there was nothing he could do short of turning the ship around and returning to Egypt, which luckily for me did not seem a reasonable option. Safely out of Egypt, I finally got my cabin.

I had no luggage but I had some money, and at the ship's small store I bought the basic necessities for the five-day voyage ahead. In many ways, that December 9th was the day of my rebirth, a day I will never forget.[25]

My cabin on the *Esperia* became my sanctuary, and for the first three days of my journey I slept more than 12 hours a day. For the first time in months, I felt free, not in the way I felt before I was first arrested in France, but free just knowing that I was safely out of Egypt and on my way to be with my mother.

Although I longed for my love Adele to be there with me, I was sure I would see her soon. By then she had secured a job in the United States, so we just needed to get there, marry and start our new life together. But that would have to wait, as I needed to focus on helping my mother.

Because there were only 14 first-class passengers, we all ate at one table, and on the second day of the five-day journey, I met a young married

---

[25] As was the day I went up Mount Arafat in Saudi Arabia in 2008, in fulfilment of my *hajj* pilgrimage obligations. Standing on Mount Arafat waiting for the sun to rise was a spiritual experience, as was climbing into bed in my ship cabin at about 3 pm with the expectation of starting a new life in America. They were very different feelings – yet somehow they seemed to be connected.

Austrian woman who was maybe five or six years older than I was and was also travelling first class. She was stunning. With red hair and green eyes, she had no trouble standing out from the rest of the passengers. As befitting a luxury liner in 1961, an orchestra aboard the *Esperia* played for the passengers after dinner, and this mysterious Austrian woman and I danced together. Although Adele was never far from my mind, even though I was still quite naïve about such things, I soon realised that the Austrian was coming on to me. I was unsure how to handle the situation without causing offence, and I tried over and over to explain that I was not available. I'm in love with someone else, I said. I'm engaged. I'm going to be married.

Eventually the woman seemed to understand but pressed me to go to Austria with her, at which point I felt I needed to explain that after getting to Italy, I was indeed planning to continue on to Austria, although I did not tell her that my reason for heading to Austria was to pick up some suitcases that Willie Hendrix, the man who had hired me as executor for the Pinto family, had left for me there.

The woman persisted. Her car was on the ship, she said. Why didn't we get off in Genoa together, visit Milan and then go to Vienna? I explained that I was meeting my mother in Milan (though still not trusting this woman, I omitted the reason), and although she continued to pester me, I finally rejected her proposals and advances.

Thanks to my Italian visa I had no problem entering the country, and when we finally disembarked the *Esperia*, I said goodbye to the Austrian woman, breathed a sigh of relief and took a train to Milan.

My trip to Austria was not without excitement; to my great surprise and dismay, the Austrian woman continued to pester me, showing up at my hotel and insisting on driving me to Vienna. Again I said no, but again she would not give up. So eventually I found myself in her car, not sure what to do with this slightly frightening, slightly intriguing woman. I was dressed in thin clothes, thin shoes, and a very thin top coat, an outfit better suited to Egypt than a car trip across the Alps from Italy into Austria. Sure enough, we encountered snow and ice and had car trouble bad enough to force us to spend two nights together while the car was being repaired. The Austrian woman could not be reasoned with and kept pursuing me, making sexual advances and pressing me to marry her. She could petition for Austrian citizenship for me, she said. She had all the money we could possibly need, and I could continue my studies. Her husband had converted all his money into gold, she said, and the gold was hidden in the car's doors. Again and again I refused. I was going to marry Adele, I said. I wanted nothing to do with this woman or her money. And I remained faithful to Adele.

I was immensely relieved when we finally reached Vienna, where I collected the suitcases that Willie Hendrix had left for me. Back in Milan, I was finally reunited with my mother, who seemed jovial despite her illness and the challenges ahead. On 16 December 1961, my mother and I boarded the *Cristoforo Colombo*, bound for the United States, where I was determined to see that she got the best possible treatment.

January–February 1962:
New York and Indianapolis

MY MOTHER AND I disembarked the *Cristoforo Colombo* on a brisk morning and checked into the hotel she had booked, the Sherry-Netherland on Fifth Avenue, across from the main entrance to Central Park. It was close to the Park Hotel, where we had stayed in 1947 on our way to Brazil, where my father had been stationed as a diplomat. Since not much had changed during these years, I remembered the area and found pleasure watching the shoppers on Fifth Avenue. My mother soon learned that her husband, Howard, would be in the hospital in Indianapolis for several days, getting treatment for a kidney infection. He insisted that we stay, and so we wound up spending a week in New York.

I was doggedly determined to finish my law degree, and during our time in New York I contacted friends from Egypt who were earning their masters and doctorates at Harvard Law School. One was kind enough to talk on my behalf to the assistant dean, to whom I sent my academic papers, which I had mailed from Egypt, anticipating a need such as this. I was admitted into the master's programme but soon realised that if I stayed in the United States, I could not practice law without a full law degree or with a foreign degree, so I needed to get a US law degree. Harvard accepted me into its JD programme, giving me a semester's credit for my Egyptian degree and for my studies at Dijon University in France and the University of Geneva in Switzerland. That was not much, and there was the problem of the high tuition fees, which I could not afford.

My mother, who was well off after buying some property in Manhattan in the late 1930s, when my father had been vice-consul of Egypt, offered to pay my fees. But I had my pride. I didn't want anyone to say that I had come to the United States so my mother could pay for my American law degree. I figured I could ask her for a loan, but given her diagnosis, chances were that by the time I finished my studies and was able to start paying her back, she would be gone. As a young man, these bursts of pride made it hard for me to think reasonably.

During our New York stay my mother arranged for me to have lunch with her attorney, who worked at an old Manhattan law firm and had steered her toward buying the downtown property. He was a Harvard graduate and took me to the Harvard Club. As we were about to be seated, he spotted a classmate sitting with another gentleman. Both New York lawyers seemed to understand that they were with guests whose company they did not necessarily expect to enjoy, so they decided we should all sit together.

The two Harvard lawyers talked with each other. The other guest, a congenial and gregarious man who stood more than six feet tall, had an accent that I later found out was a Hoosier's, meaning he was from Indiana. He asked what I was doing, and I told him about my quandary about Harvard Law School: should I get a JD, which would require two and a half years, or an LLM, which would take only a year and a half? Money, I said, was a big concern.

To my astonishment, he suggested I attend Indiana University, where I could have a full scholarship. When I looked confused, he explained that he was dean of the law school. I soon realised that attending law school in Indianapolis would mean that I could live at my mother's house, study without incurring any debt, and work part-time to pay for my personal expenses. It was everything I could hope for and more.

I immediately accepted the dean's offer, not wanting him to have any time to reconsider. On the way back to the hotel, I wondered: what were the chances that at lunch at the Harvard Club in New York I would meet the dean of a law school in Indianapolis, where my mother lived, and he would offer me a free ride to attend school there? I thanked the Lord until I got to the hotel and told my mother, who jumped with joy.

After a few days of eating, shopping and enjoying the sights and sounds of New York City, Howard called my mother to let her know he was out of the hospital and back home recovering. I had met Howard almost a year earlier when he visited Egypt with my mother, and I knew he was a very affable, warm, kind person. We got along well. After the call, my mother and I packed our bags and travelled to Indianapolis.

Winter 1975: Chicago

A S I CONTINUED to think about the relationship between Egypt and Israel during 1974 and 1975, the topic came home to me both personally and academically. My involvement intensified in Chicago sometime in early 1975, when Abba Eban, who had been Israel's minister of foreign affairs from 1966 to 1974, gave a speech at the Chicago Council on Foreign Relations. After the speech, I was invited to a private dinner hosted by a Chicago banker where I met Morton Kaplan, who at the time was the head of the Center for Strategic Studies at the University of Chicago.

Kaplan was a brilliant political scientist, and we immediately hit it off intellectually, although we were very different temperamentally. He was a pure academic who at times appeared to have no interests in life other than his work, which made him seem slightly antisocial, while I was comparatively open, sociable and even voluble. I also had more political experience, which, along with my familiarity with diplomats and their world because of my father's work, helped me better understand how to put ideas into effect.

Soon after the dinner, Kaplan and I met at his University of Chicago office and found ourselves amicably role-playing peace-treaty negotiations: he represented Israel, and I represented Egypt. Before getting into specifics, we agreed that we had to settle on basic principles – for me, a jurist, and for Kaplan, a political scientist, this was a natural beginning. It took us only a few hours to agree on basic principles, a task I felt was somewhat reminiscent of President Woodrow Wilson's creation of the 1918 Fourteen Points that became the basis for peace in Europe, the Treaty of Versailles, and the establishment of the League of Nations.

Kaplan and I then returned to our respective offices, and after a few days we faxed back and forth the text of our different formulations of the principles. From there, we proceeded to write a brief commentary on each principle. When we were finished, Kaplan arranged for their publication under the auspices of the Center for Strategic Studies of the University of Chicago as a booklet titled *A Mideast Proposal*.[26]

---

[26] M Cherif Bassiouni and Morton Kaplan, *A Mideast Proposal* (Monograph, The University of Chicago, 1975).

We submitted this to the Senate Committee on Foreign Relations on 23 July 1975. On the same day, I testified before a Foreign Relations subcommittee as part of hearings entitled 'The Arab–Israeli Dispute – Priorities for Peace'.[27]

[27] I testified before the subcommittee on Near Eastern and South Asian Affairs of the Committee on Foreign Relations, at the hearings on the Middle East entitled 'The Arab–Israeli Dispute – Priorities for Peace'. Letter on file with author (at DePaul University from John Sparkman, chairman of US Senate Committee on Foreign Relations, letter sent 18 July 1975).

January–April 1962: Indianapolis

SHORTLY AFTER RETURNING to Indianapolis, my mother asked me to go with her to see the Indianapolis attorney handling her husband Howard's business, a company called Robot Salesman Inc. The company manufactured revolving advertising signs, designed to attract the attention of passing motorists, that were placed in the parking lots of car dealerships, restaurants and other places of business. The advertising signs, which were 10–12 feet in diameter, could have different and changing messages that could be read at some distance. It was something I knew nothing about and had no interest in. What I did not know was that my mother had heavily invested in the company, as had a classmate of Howard's, a wealthy landowner from Kokomo, Indiana. When my mother, the man from Kokomo and I met with the attorney, we were shocked to hear that the company was on the verge of bankruptcy.

We discussed the company's precarious financial situation for about two hours. Finally, the attorney came up with a proposal: if the investors, my mother and the man from Kokomo, found a manager who could enhance sales and improve manufacturing, perhaps the company could survive. Neither investor had any idea where to find such a manager, especially on such short notice, and they were quiet until my mother turned to me and almost yelled. 'Mouky', she said, using the nickname she always called me by, 'You can do it!'

The two other gentlemen looked at me incredulously – with good reason. How could a foreigner, an Egyptian who was only 24 years old, with a strong accent and no business experience in the United States, manage a company? But my mother, after recounting some of my business exploits in Egypt, insisted I could save this company. I demurred – without realising that in the process, as I described the company's problems and why I was not the person to solve them, I was telling them exactly what needed to be done.

The next day I went to the factory to take over as acting president and found three blue-collar workers, two salesmen and a secretary, all of whom were hostile, if not derisive, toward me. I quickly realised that they seemed to have been operating under some very lax rules, with each doing what he or she wanted when he or she wanted to do it. But I was from Egypt, where hierarchy was important not just in social settings.

In Egypt, people did what they were told, not what they wanted to. Having been in a managerial capacity before, I understood that part of the problem.

That first day, I asked one of the salesmen and one of the workers to wait outside while I talked to the others. I told the others that I needed to learn more about the business before developing new policies and practices and that I looked forward to their cooperation and support. I then dismissed the group and invited the two others in, one at a time, and told them that they were fired. That was the strongest possible message I could send to the remaining members of the staff, and from that point on, they understood that I was not simply a kid from Egypt who had just gotten off the boat and was still wet behind his ears. I was their boss, and I was going to do everything I could to make the company a success.

It was a long time, maybe six months, before I grasped all the details of manufacturing, shipping and installing the revolving signs, as well as the difficulties in selling this product throughout the Midwest. I accompanied a salesman on several trips, travelling mostly through Indiana, Ohio, parts of Kentucky, and Michigan. I learned a lot about the United States and about the toughness of its merchants and businesspeople and was able to keep the company just about afloat from month to month.

But I knew that the company could not last long in this month-to-month limbo and that something needed to happen to ensure its survival. So one day, on a hunch, I wrote to the vice-president and general manager of the Ford Motor division, a Mr Lee Iacocca. I told Iacocca about the product we manufactured and that I would like to try a leasing programme with ten company-owned dealerships in various parts of the United States that he would designate, to try to measure whether our revolving signs enhanced Ford's sales.

The letter must have caught Iacocca's attention because I was invited to meet with a senior person in Detroit and made my first trip to that city. To my surprise, a week later I received confirmation of the ten-unit lease in various parts of Michigan, Indiana, Ohio and Illinois. I was elated: we produced about one unit a month, and now we had a contract for ten. The problem was, how could we finance buying the equipment necessary to transport the units to the locations and install them? I had no money and didn't know where to get funding, but somebody mentioned a company in Chicago that specialised in funding leases and retail contracts. I wrote a letter to the chairman of the board, attaching my letter to Iacocca and the response of one of his executives. Again, to my surprise, I was invited to meet with the lender in Chicago, where, after a half-hour meeting, the chairman turned me over to one of his vice-presidents with a simple order: 'Fund him.' (I think the lender, a well-established business personality who happened to be Jewish, perhaps was intrigued to receive such a letter from a young Muslim immigrant from Egypt.) That is how Robot Salesman Inc. fulfilled the Ford contract and I saved the company. I was certainly developing a taste for the American dream.

March–April 1962: District of Columbia, United States

J UST A FEW months after arriving in the United States and starting to settle down in Indianapolis, I had an extraordinary American experience.

Because my father had been Egypt's ambassador to India at the same time that Chester Bowles, the former governor of Connecticut, was serving in the same post for the United States, I got a letter of introduction from my father to Bowles that I sent him upon my arrival in Indianapolis. At the time, he was the special representative and adviser on African, Asian and Latin American affairs and ambassador-at-large to President John F. Kennedy. Bowles was not only a prominent politician in the Democratic Party; he was a wealthy businessman who owned Benton & Bowles, one of the country's largest advertising agencies.

In late March or early April 1962, Bowles received me in his office in what I believe is called the executive part of the White House, which was very exciting for a young man so recently arrived from so far away. Just as we were exchanging the usual pleasantries, the door of his office burst open and a man in a white shirt with an open tie and rolled-up sleeves and a distinctive Boston accent barged in, demanding a report on Yugoslavia from the State Department.

Then President Kennedy noticed that somebody else was in the office, turned toward me, and said, 'I apologize for the interruption.' Bowles made the introduction, telling the president that I was the son of Egypt's former ambassador to India who had recently moved to the United States from Egypt to study law. Hearing that, JFK looked at me profoundly, shook my hand a second time, and said, 'Welcome to the United States.' I have no idea how many immigrants have been personally welcomed by the president, but from that moment on, I thought there was no limit to what I could accomplish in this country. (I was taken down a notch – and received a lesson in politics – a few months later, however, when Kennedy stopped in Indianapolis on a campaign visit. Even though I was not a US citizen, I went to the airport with about 300 other Democrats to greet him. I stood by the rope line and shook his hand, and he showed no sign of recognition.)

February–December 1962:
Indianapolis and Chicago

M Y FIRST MONTHS in Indianapolis were filled with work for a company I really was not interested in – and extreme heartbreak. Not long after I arrived in the United States, the American journalist I had encountered the day I met Adele at the US embassy in Cairo delivered bad news: shortly after I had left Egypt, he said, Adele's father became very ill and died. Her widowed mother was old, sick and depressed, and because Adele's brother and sister-in-law were leaving Egypt soon to move to the United States, Adele had decided not to emigrate.

I felt as if I were going to collapse. After we had worked so hard to keep our relationship alive despite our religious differences, after we had made so many plans for our future, after she had gotten herself a job in Washington, DC, and I had moved to Indianapolis, just when it looked as if our dreams could actually come true, Adele was not coming to the United States. I wrote to her several times, but each letter went unanswered.

I fell into a deep depression. Despite my wish to forget about the world around me, I had no choice but to continue my work at Robot Salesman as well as start classes at Indiana University School of Law at Indianapolis in June 1962. I was working all day, going to school from 6 to 8.30 pm, and then going home to have dinner and study for the next day or prepare to drive throughout the Midwest for work. This is when I started drinking. I drank during the evenings, after I returned from law school while studying for the next day's classes. I drank on the weekends. Not being much of a drinker before then, the alcohol had quite an effect, and I found myself in such a depressed state that I cried almost every evening and on the weekends.

I had no idea that I could go to a psychologist or psychiatrist, start therapy and get some medication. That was totally alien to my background. But I forced myself to focus on my education, and slowly the pain of my heartbreak began to fade and I found myself more engaged in my law school life and where I would go from there.

I also found myself in a new relationship. When I was arranging my departure from Egypt, because I had not expected to meet my mother in Milan and sail to New York with her, I had bought a one-way ticket for an Alitalia flight from Milan to New York. By the autumn of 1962, settled into my new life in the United States and having no need for the ticket, I called Alitalia's Chicago office to inquire about a refund. The office manager insisted that she could not refund a non-refundable ticket but also said that I was welcome to come to Chicago and argue my case in person.

I did so a few weeks later, combining the trip with a visit to my mother and cousin, who were staying in Chicago, and arriving late on a Friday, a few minutes after the office had closed. A woman I assumed to be the office manager was sitting at her desk across from two men, and she let me in and introduced me to the two men (one of whom, maestro Bruno Bartoletti, later became a friend and associate) before they left. After listening to my account of why I had travelled to New York by ship, the manager held firm: because the non-refundable ticket had been issued in Cairo, I could not get my money back. By that time, it was almost 6 pm, and because I felt bad about keeping her in the office so late, I invited her to dinner with my mother and my cousin, who was studying for an MBA in Chicago. She agreed.

In the months that followed, the manager, Rossana, and I spent more time together. I visited her in Chicago, and she came to Indianapolis. Our relationship soon became more serious, and we decided to marry. I was still mourning the loss of Adele and in a depressed, post-traumatic state, fearing that Egyptian intelligence would send someone to assassinate me, even in Indianapolis, but I thought marriage was for the best. We were married in Chicago on 17 December, just a few months after meeting in Alitalia's office.

My mother did not stay in the area long; shortly after I moved to Indianapolis, her husband, Howard, passed away, and she soon moved to California.

April 1993: Geneva

THE WORK OF the Commission of Experts in the former Yugoslavia was well under way when I was summoned to New York City to meet with UN Secretary-General Boutros Boutros-Ghali, an old friend. On the journey, with the commission's work in mind, I wondered: why does history include so many atrocities and tragedies, events in which we destroy and demean each other and lose sight of our common human bond?

My meeting with Boutros Boutros-Ghali provided a kind of answer, at least to the question of why we lose sight of human dignity and human worth: the secretary-general chastised me for being too zealous in trying to bringing to light the atrocities of the ongoing conflict. Boutros Boutros-Ghali strongly supported me and my work, but he was clearly receiving political pressure. He wanted me to be more cautious. 'You have a beautiful office in Geneva', he said. 'Stay in it. Keep your back to the wall, avoid political criticism, stay neutral, and stay out of the field.'

This was the language of a different universe, the one on the 38th floor of the UN headquarters overlooking the East River in New York. This was not the universe of Poljana Pakračka and so many similar places I had visited. I was shocked and bewildered, not yet having learned how to shift my emotional and intellectual gears. These words had nothing to do with the ongoing conflict in the former Yugoslavia, where innocent civilians were killed largely because of their religious or ethnic affiliations, nothing to do with the ethnic cleansing and mass rape we were investigating. I tucked the secretary-general's statement into the back of my mind, intending it to remind me what the commission was up against, beyond the conflict and all that it brought with it, but I was even more steadfast in my determination to see the commission succeed.

May 1964: Chicago

BEFORE GRADUATING FROM law school, as a member and vice-justice of the Phi Alpha Delta law fraternity, I attended a conclave in Chicago, where I met a man named Albert Vail, who turned out to be a law professor at DePaul University, a private Catholic university in Chicago. We developed a good rapport, and he told me to call him the next time I was in Chicago.

After I got a job at an insurance company in Chicago shortly before graduation, Rossana and I made the move to Chicago. Once I settled into my new position, I followed up on Al Vail's invitation, and we met for lunch. He brought along his former law partner, Philip Romiti, who turned out to be the dean of DePaul's law school. I genuinely enjoyed the company of these two men, although I had no idea of their roles at DePaul. We lost track of time, and before hurriedly leaving, Romiti told me my contract would arrive within a couple of weeks. 'You're a great guy', he said. 'I look forward to having you on the faculty. When you get the contract, call me and we will talk about the courses.'

I had no idea what he was talking about and was even more surprised when Vail extended his hand and said in his warm, quiet voice, 'Welcome to DePaul University College of Law.' I was shocked – I had thought this was just a nice lunch between new friends, in no way suspecting it was any type of interview – much less an interview for a job I never applied for.

Vail's explanation came in the form of story. Vail was an American historian, and every summer he followed a historic trail, one dating from the early settling of the American West, from the Midwest to the West Coast. Vail liked to drive the trail as if he were a settler, although his journey was not filled with much hardship, as he travelled in an air-conditioned car and stayed at comfortable hotels along the way. He told me about a spot at the end of the trail in California where the wagon trails would break up and different wagons would go to various towns to settle. As the story went, an older man was always there when the wagon trains arrived, and he would walk up and down the line, talking to the travellers, asking where they had come from and whether they had left behind good family and friends. If travellers told him that they had no relatives back home or that their family and neighbours were best forgotten, the man urged them to keep going. But, the story said, if someone spoke fondly of those they had left behind and those who had helped them along the way, he urged them to come to his town. Vail then looked at me. I had experienced much hardship, he said, but I seldom spoke ill of people, and I always remembered the help and support I got from others. That, he said, is the type of person he and others at DePaul wanted in their community. Learning how to teach criminal law is not a big deal, he said, but being a good and decent person is.

The decision took me a little time, but I eventually decided to take a chance, leave my job and try teaching. I had no clue that it would be the beginning of 45 years teaching at DePaul.

My first few years at DePaul were a challenge, mostly because I had never taught before. In those years, I taught several sections of criminal law, a subject I had not enjoyed very much in my own studies. I also was the faculty member responsible for overseeing the second-year students' appellate brief writing, and I participated on several school committees. In those days, people in academia were expected to put in a full day's work, including a heavy load of classroom teaching, and I found myself with a nine-hour course load. Nine hours in the classroom was only the beginning; I had to prepare for each class, take time to meet with my students, and participate in school committees and public service. I was also expected to publish scholarly articles (and later books) on a regular basis.

The commitment was great, the pay low. My salary that first year of teaching in 1964 was $8,500 a year, and it was four years more before I was earning $12,000 per year, which was the insurance company salary I had given up to take the job at DePaul. Promotions at DePaul were generally slow in coming; on average, associate professors took 10–12 years to make full professor. Fortunately for me, I published my first textbook, *Criminal Law and its Processes: The Law of Public Order*, in 1969, after only five years of teaching, and I was promoted to full professor that same year.

My first published piece, in the *DePaul Law Review Journal* in 1965, came just a year after I joined the DePaul faculty: a revision of my paper for Paul Guggenheim on the legality of the nationalisation of the Suez Canal.

* * *

In those early days at DePaul, the staff and faculty were close-knit. After I arrived, I quickly learned that Vail's description was accurate.

In the DePaul community, people shared hopes and expectations as well as disappointments and losses, and it quickly became a new family for me. I fondly remember faculty and staff meals on the fourth floor and in the staff dining room at the Law Center: many of us would sit around the large round table with colleagues as well as the university's seniors, president, executive vice-present, chancellor and others. Our conversations were lively and open, with no subject off-limits. We could question, discuss and criticise university policies and practices. Just as I had at Dijon University, in the DePaul community I learned from others' successes, accomplishments and challenges.

My decision to go into legal education brought highs and lows, and one of the lows was financial. With my small salary, the only way I could make ends meet was to practice law, so during the first few years I worked with an acquaintance in a private practice, renting two offices in downtown Chicago. My colleague and I did everything that came through the door: contracts, wills, trusts, divorce and personal injury litigation.

In my early years at DePaul I worked on a large number of cases deriving from the mass arrests in the 1968 Chicago riots and arrests in connection with the 1968 Democratic convention anti-Vietnam protests. These pro bono experiences, which forced me to into a courtroom, taught me how important it is to link theory to practice. I found it exhilarating and moved on from there to engage in limited but varied legal practice. My work in these areas, which extended to real estate transactions, immigration work, divorce matters, criminal defence, international business transactions and even a few personal injury matters, had more to do with supplementing my income at the time (which was hardly enough to live on) than gaining experience.

During my first two years teaching at DePaul, I also earned my master's of law degree from John Marshall Law School. Later, I devoted a significant amount of my attention to the specialised field of international extradition, a topic I first became interested in as a result of my efforts to prevent the extradition of the Pinto family by Egypt from Italy. Twenty years later, I had worked on more than 100 such cases, including those of foreign heads of state, members of cabinets, and well-known businesspeople. This also led me to the same type of work in more than 30 European countries, introducing me to a network that became an essential resource.

In part this was due to the fact that my first book on extradition, *International Extradition: US Law and Practice*, the only one in the United States since J.B. Moore's 1891 work *A Treatise on Extradition and Inter-State Rendition*, was frequently cited by the courts. Extradition was pivotal to international comparative law in the Cold War climate, as each nation sought to shield its citizens from an antagonistic criminal system, and my legal education in America and Europe afforded me a strong base of knowledge in other legal codes.

After my first decade of teaching, I decided to further pursue my own academic studies and enrolled in the doctor of juridical science programme at George Washington University in Washington, DC. There I wrote my dissertation on extradition, and in 1974 I went on to publish my work as a book on the subject. My work on extradition, one of the few of its kind, was well received and frequently cited.

April 1997: Chicago, Ottowa, New York

IN MOST OF the extradition and mutual legal assistance cases in which I was involved, I served as an expert witness for the principal defence counsel in the case. Every case featured an important legal principle, one that I believed extended to everyone, even those we think of as evil or criminal, such as members of the Mafia or accused terrorists. The US Constitution makes no such distinction.

Two particular cases stand out in my mind. In the first, I was appointed the legal expert for the government of Canada to show that the international crime known as crimes against humanity was illegal during the time at issue. In the other, I stood up for the political-offence exception in the extradition defence of Mousa Abu Marzook, one of the political leaders of the group Hamas who was, at the time, a legal permanent resident of the United States.

In 1987, the Canadian government amended its Criminal Code to make war crimes and crimes against humanity offences that could be tried in a Canadian court, even if they were committed outside Canada and even if the crimes happened before the amendments were adopted. This law was passed in response to growing evidence and public concern that many former Nazis had escaped responsibility for their crimes by hiding in the West and that the countries where they lived showed little interest in or capability for holding these individuals to account.

The Canadian legislation, however, required proving that the crime in question existed in international law – and under Canadian criminal law – at the time it was committed. The connection to Canadian law was not difficult to prove, but establishing the existence of crimes against humanity in international law was daunting. How could I show that an international customary law, with respect to crimes against humanity, existed before it was embodied in the Statute of the International Military Tribunal (better known as the Nuremberg trials)? The crimes involved in the Canadian prosecutions all happened before June 1945. As Canada's chief legal expert, I needed to prove the existence of crimes against humanity before the Nuremberg Charter was signed as a treaty in London on 8 August 1945.

The first case was brought by the Canadian government in 1989 against Imre Finta, a former captain of the Royal Hungarian Gendarmerie, which was a paramilitary federal police force with responsibility for law and order in the Hungarian countryside. Captain Finta was assigned to Szeged, near where the Hungarian, Romanian and Yugoslavian borders met, with instructions to carry out the Baky Order, a decree issued by the Hungarian interior ministry calling for the isolation, expropriation, ghettoisation concentration, and eventual deportation of all Hungarian Jews. Beginning in June of 1944, Captain Finta gathered 8,617 Jews in a brickyard in Szeged, mostly the elderly, women and children, since most of the able-bodied men had either been taken or induced to work in German factories. The victims were then stripped of their valuables and loaded into those now-infamous railway waggons in inhumane conditions for the five-day journey to Austria and then to Auschwitz, Poland.

Captain Finta's whereabouts in the immediate aftermath of the Axis defeat is unknown, but in 1947 he was tried in absentia in Hungary and convicted of 'crimes against the people' in relation to the mass deportation of Szeged's Jewish population in the summer of 1944. In 1951, however, Captain Finta immigrated to Canada. He became a Canadian citizen five years later.

In 1989, I was well established as an authority on international criminal law, but I was still somewhat surprised to be chosen by the Canadian Ministry of Justice to fill the dual role of advising the Canadian prosecution team and helping prepare its legal arguments and also testifying at the trial as the chief legal expert. This was, after all, a case driven by facts, and I would have expected the Canadian government to choose an expert who was more familiar with the details of the Nazis' extermination plans in Hungary. I later learned that in the eyes of the Canadian ministry, I was the perfect choice: I had substantive knowledge and a well-known commitment, and I was a foreigner, so if I failed to make the case on the law, the Canadian government couldn't be blamed. Being an Egyptian-born Arab-American Muslim, a foreigner thrice over, made me the perfect fall guy.

My problem, however, was to legally establish the existence of crimes against humanity in international law before Nuremberg. Because there had been no treaty on crimes against humanity and only an emerging custom, I was afraid the case would be weak. Then one day I thought of a theoretical basis to prove the case in a different way. One of the sources of international law is called 'general principles of law', which means that a given legal principle or legal proposition exists in all (or almost all) legal systems of the world. I expanded this beyond a mere legal principle or proposition to include specific crimes and listed the specific crimes in the category called 'crimes against humanity' as defined in the Nuremberg Charter: 'murder, extermination, deportation, enslavement, and other inhumane acts' and 'persecution'.

I listed each of these crimes and other, related ones (manslaughter, for example, would be included in 'murder', and rape would be included in 'other inhumane acts') across the top of a wide sheet of paper, in a header row. Then, in a column that stretched vertically down the left side of the page, I listed all the countries that existed in 1944, which I found to total 74. I then sent research assistants to the major law libraries in Chicago and I went to the library of Congress in Washington, looking for the criminal codes of these 74 countries that were in effect in 1944.

Looking through the codes, I confirmed what I had initially suspected: each code contained some reference to the crimes that I had listed horizontally across the page. Working across each country's row, under each crime I listed the reference to that crime in the country's criminal code. The completed chart was a clear illustration: all the codified national legal systems in existence in 1944 contained prohibitions about the same specific crimes as those that were contained in the Nuremberg Charter. This, I concluded, was evidence that the Nuremberg definition of crimes against humanity was embodied in the general principles of law of all the world's national criminal justice systems.

The next step was to solicit from experts in each of these countries an affidavit declaring that the crimes in question existed in their legal systems in 1944. This was not as easy as it sounds, and I could never have accomplished it without the connections I had developed as president of the AIDP. Even so, identifying the country experts, obtaining the affidavits, translating them into English, attaching copies of the codes, translating the codes and preparing binders of documents was a monumental task for me and my assistant and secretary. The documents, all of which had to be authenticated, filled six binders that when piled up stood more than three feet high.

My testimony and cross-examination about my legal research were supposed to take a day or perhaps a day and a half, but the defence counsel, who was reputed to be a strong supporter of neo-Nazi groups in Canada, kept me on the stand under cross-examination six hours a day for five days. The counsel's questioning, which did not show much understanding of the legal issues, seemed designed to show that I was Jewish but concealing myself as an Arab Muslim. How involved was I, he asked, in 'Jewish politics? Holocaust politics?' Eventually, I could not resist giving him a taste of his own medicine: although I was an Arab Muslim, I said,

I did have some Jewish cousins. His curiosity piqued, he pressed me to explain. I told him that I had an ancestor by the name of Abraham who had two sons, Isaac and Ismail, and that while my family came from Ismail, my cousins from Uncle Isaac were all Jewish. The reference went right over the counsel's head, but observers in the courtroom laughed loudly.

In the end, Captain Finta was acquitted under a Canadian defence that he was simply following his superiors' orders, but the new theory that I had developed, backed by the data, carried the day in court, and the judgment acknowledged that 'crimes against humanity' did exist in 1944 prior to the Nuremberg Charter. We proved a challenging legal question, and it has continued to be a significant legal precedent.

The second case, that of Mousa Abu Marzook, involved an extradition doctrine called the political-offence exception. This principle, which is written into the vast majority of extradition treaties, has roots extending back to the 16th century and the writing of Hugo Grotius, a Dutch jurist who lived from 1583 to 1645. This exception embodies many of the freedoms that American citizens are granted by the First Amendment to the Constitution, namely freedom of speech and assembly. It stands for the distinction between politics and criminality: political work is protected, whereas common crimes are not. Too much blood has been spilled historically in learning the truth that armed rebellions alone, without political negotiation, cannot bring peace and security. The political-offence exception is the recognition of this lesson: politics is ultimately the only way to resolve war. Only politics can supplant weapons with words.

In 1992, Marzook, a leader of the political wing of the Hamas movement, was placed on the US Immigration and Naturalization Service's 'watch list' of individuals suspected of terrorist activities. No charges of any kind or suggestions of wrongdoing were lodged against him. He continued to travel throughout the world extensively using his US re-entry documents, as he had been a permanent resident alien since coming to the United States to further his education in 1982. This came to an end on 25 July 1995, when at the request of the Israeli government, Marzook was detained at JFK International Airport.

Within a week, the government of Israel had requested Marzook's extradition to Israel on charges that amounted to being part of a criminal conspiracy related to 10 terrorist attacks. However, not one piece of evidence presented by either Israel or the United States clearly tied Marzook to any conspiracy or any terrorist acts in any way that should have been considered legally meaningful. While Marzook freely acknowledged his position as the head of Hamas's political bureau, neither government made a connection between the political bureau of Hamas and its military wing, known as the Qassam brigades. The segmented nature of resistance movements dates as least as far back as the early 20th century and the organisation of Sinn Féin and the Irish Republican Army. While the military wing of the movement carries out an armed struggle, the political wing carries out propaganda, political and social activities. Even the US State Department, in *Patterns of Global Terrorism: 1994*, described Hamas as 'loosely structured, with some elements working openly through mosques and social service institutions to recruit members, raise money, organize activities, and distribute propaganda'.[28] And that while 'various elements of Hamas have used both peaceful and violent means, including terrorism ... it has also engaged in peaceful political activity, such as running candidates in the West Bank Chamber of Commerce elections'.[29]

My work on the Marzook case involved helping with strategy and briefs. Whatever the legal and evidentiary merits of the case, the US government found a pair of receptive judges in Kevin Duffy and Kimba Wood, who were happy to overlook the clear language of the US law, the US–Israel extradition treaty and decades of American legal precedent.

After more than 18 months in solitary confinement in the Metropolitan Correctional Center of New York, on 28 January 1997, Marzook decided that facing trial in Israel was preferable to spending the indeterminate future in a US jail and agreed to extradition to Israel. While this should have been the end of the issue, the Israeli government was then in the position of the proverbial dog that has caught the car: having produced no evidence to prove a connection between Marzook and the militant wing of Hamas, how was it going to put him on trial in Israel? The answer turned out to be that it was not. On 3 April 1997, after Marzook had spent 21 months in jail, the Israeli government dropped its extradition request rather than chance the ignominy of losing a highly publicised case in Israel.

The United States, having made such a clear showing of its belief that Marzook was connected to militant terrorism, now also had to try to save face. So the Immigration and Naturalization Service moved to revoke Marzook's resident-alien status and have him expelled from the United States. Rather than put up with being detained further, Marzook

---

[28] US Department of State, *Patterns of Global Terrorism: 1994*, no 10239 (1995) 41, available at https://www.hsdl.org/?view&did=481511.
[29] Ibid.

renounced his resident alien status and was eventually flown to Jordan. Adding insult to injury, the US government flew him to Amman on a military aircraft, shackled and wearing an orange jumpsuit.

Hence Mousa Abu Marzook, much like Bruno Pinto, the man whose circumstances first prompted my interest in the topic of extradition, was forced to leave his life behind and start all over in a new land.

1970s–1990s: Chicago and Various Cities Throughout the World

CONSIDERING MY LIFE experiences – being raised in a family with a long history of supporting the Egyptian state, serving in the Egyptian National Guard in the Suez, being arrested first for days in France and then for months in Egypt, and wanting to protect those who were mistreated by security forces – those who knew me were not surprised that from the start of my time at DePaul I would specialise in international criminal law and human rights, working with as much enthusiasm and vigour as I could muster for the advancement of human rights and international criminal law. I travelled often to speak at conferences, wrote more and more journal articles and books on these subjects, and served in scholarly and professional organisations. At first, the results were modest. I was young and without academic standing, and, as I later discovered, being of Arab origin and being a Muslim were big handicaps.

May 1993–July 1994:
Chicago and The Hague

OF ALL THE awards and honours I have been fortunate to receive, I have always considered the Outstanding New Citizen of the Year Award, which I received in 1967, one of those I am most proud of.

Citizenship was always a goal. After arriving in the United States in the first month of 1962, I started the work of becoming a naturalised US citizen, a process I completed five years later. On 18 September 1967, to my great pleasure, I not only became a full citizen; I received the Outstanding New Citizen of the Year Award from the Citizenship Council of Metropolitan Chicago. Ten thousand people were naturalized in the Chicago area that year, and I was honoured to be chosen from that number to address a crowd of more than 5,000 people gathered for the swearing-in of 1,200 new citizens.

My swearing-in ceremony and my selection to speak that day symbolised my becoming an official member of my new country, and it also solidified my new home at DePaul University. Among the families, friends and community members of new citizens present at the event were many members of the DePaul community, all there to support me: the president of the university, Revd John Cortelyou, and the then-dean of the College of Law, Philip Romiti, whom I had met at that fortuitous lunch just a few years before, presented me with my award. I truly felt that I was at home in this new country, in Chicago and at DePaul.

* * *

By the spring of 1993, however, many in the international community seemed oblivious to my decades as a proud American citizen.

The Commission of Experts' First Interim Report on its investigation in the territory of the former Yugoslavia had moved the international community to take historical measures and establish the International Criminal Tribunal for the Former Yugoslavia (ICTY) to prosecute those responsible for the commission of war crimes and crimes against humanity in the region. After the ICTY was officially established by Security

Council Resolution 827 in May 1993, the next step was to staff the tribunal. But despite the international community's agreement on the decision to establish such a tribunal, throughout its creation *realpolitik* prevailed.

One of the biggest decisions in designing the tribunal was finding the right person to serve at its chief prosecutor. The prosecutor is an important role in any judicial institution, but it was even more so for the ICTY, as this was the first international criminal tribunal since Nuremburg, and the whole world was watching. This decision was left to the UN Security Council, and in August 1993, my name was put forth for the position by UN Secretary-General Boutros Boutros-Ghali.[30] I had long dreamed of such a job, and I was very pleased.

Boutros Boutros-Ghali was clear: he wanted me as chief prosecutor for the newly established tribunal and nobody else. Madeleine Albright, the US ambassador to the United Nations, chaired that session at the Security Council and called me before it to say that the council was divided on my nomination but that she could fairly assure me that if I withdrew my candidacy for prosecutor, I would be guaranteed election to judgeship on the ICTY. I refused, explaining that I could not sit as a fair and impartial judge when cases arising out of matters I had investigated in the field for two years were brought to trial. I knew that the answer to such a question for most would have been easy: accept the position, recuse yourself from any matter involving your previous work, and then stay home and collect your generous under-secretary-general's tax-free salary. This is how politics and the UN bureaucracy work hand in hand to let the major powers achieve their goals.

Ambassador Albright was kind enough to thank me for all my efforts. Soon enough, I learned the result of the informal vote, held before any formal UN Security Council vote. The results were seven to seven, with the United States leading the 'yes' contingent and the United Kingdom leading the opposition. Brazil was the only country to abstain, in effect making the vote inoperative. I was crushed.

---

[30] On 26 August 1993, UN Secretary-General Boutros Boutros-Ghali sent a letter to US Ambassador Madeleine Albright in her capacity as president of the Security Council. It stated, in part, 'In view of the need for the Tribunal to be composed as soon as possible I now, pursuant to the mandate entrusted to me under 16(4), submit to you and through you to the Security Council the name of Dr Cherif Bassiouni as my nominee and ask the Council to appoint him Prosecutor of the International Tribunal. Please accept, Madame President, the assurances of my highest consideration', letter from Boutros Boutros-Ghali, UN Secretary-General, to Madeleine Albright, President of the United Nations Security Council (26 August 1993) available at https://digital.case.edu/downloads/83380n69r.

Along with all other *New York Times* readers, I soon learned the reasoning behind my rejection from an interview with Ambassador David Hannay, who was then the permanent representative of the United Kingdom to the United Nations. An article based on this interview stated (and its writer confirmed to me, along with his outrage at the situation) that Hannay and others had voted against me simply because I was a Muslim.[31] I was upset, as were other members of the international community, but there was nothing I could do about the decision. I once again felt the frustration and sadness of being judged not on my credentials or my efforts, or even my citizenship, but on my religion.

Shortly thereafter, in July 1994, the Security Council nominated and confirmed Richard Goldstone of South Africa as chief prosecutor of the ICTY. Goldstone and I had our first formal meeting at the ICTY temporary offices two days after he arrived in The Hague. Aside from new furniture, his office and its walls were bare, but within minutes three colleagues and I had spread out maps to show him the lay of the land, who and where the warring factions were, how many militia groups were engaged in actual violence, and much more. We spent the next three days briefing Goldstone and his staff and bringing them up to date, in the end supplying all our reports, data and analysis, material that consisted of 3,200 pages of information supported by 76,000 documents, more than 300 hours of video, and 3,000 photographs. We talked about the major issues of command structures, economic interests, political agendas, ethnic cleansing, systematic rape, and other ways in which war crimes and crimes against humanity were committed. Goldstone thanked us profusely and invited us to small-group meetings to expand on our findings and methodology. In many ways, we had passed the baton.

[31] Paul Lewis, 'Disputes Hamper UN Drive for a War Crimes Tribunal' *New York Times*, 9 September 1993, www.nytimes.com/1993/09/09/world/disputes-hamper-un-drive-for-a-war-crimes-tribunal.html.

1969–1975: Chicago and Siracusa

DURING THIS PERIOD, I became more involved with the work of the AIDP. Now the most prestigious international law organisation, the AIDP was founded in Vienna in 1889 and reorganised in Paris in 1924 after World War One; its members have historically been academic and policy leaders at the forefront of international law.

I had learned about the organisation from Dean Graven at the University of Geneva, and in 1968 I was contacted by Gerhard O.W. Mueller, a distinguished German-born international-law expert who held many posts, including vice-president of the AIDP, on behalf of the US national section. The US section required a *rapporteur* on extradition for its participation in the upcoming 1969 International Penal Conference, and on the strength of my interest in and work on the topic, I was asked to join. I found that being a professor and having an active law practice helped me contribute significantly to the organisation, and thus began my long and fruitful relationship with the AIDP.

In 1972, although still just a young member, I was elected deputy secretary-general of the AIDP. I was approached by Giovanni Leone, the former president of the organisation's Italian National Section who had recently been elected president of Italy, for some advice. What could he do for the AIDP that would bring credit to Italy?

I suggested something I had been pondering for a while, prompted by what I considered a dismal side effect of the Cold War: a freeze not only on communication and cooperation between the East and West but on international criminal law development. Why not establish an international centre that could serve as a rallying place for scholars, experts, researchers and students from north, south, east and west? The basic values of such a centre, I explained, would be universal humanism, and those involved with it would reach around the globe to build understanding, enhance peace, reduce conflict and the human tragedies that it brings, work to control and prevent crime, promote victims' rights, support the integrity of justice systems, and improve the administration of criminal justice. In short, the centre's goal would be to uphold human rights and preserve the rule of law.

Most of my colleagues considered these goals wildly unrealistic and attributed the idea of a global centre seeking to achieve such lofty aspirations to my personal ambitions, if not my megalomania. But I and several others were undeterred, and in conjunction with the AIDP, by September 1972 the International Institute of Higher Studies in Criminal Sciences, now known as the Siracusa Institute (or the Siracusa International Institute for Criminal Justice and Human Rights) had been established. The Sicilian city of Siracusa, which was founded by the Greeks more than 2,500 years ago, proved a perfect location. In the middle of the Mediterranean and far from any major political centre, it remains an ideal place for uniting people interested in the pursuit of international criminal justice. The city's charming history and stunning beauty do not hurt either.

The institute's work was slow at first, as it sought to establish itself and develop an international reputation. But things soon began to pick up, and the institute's work far exceeded my original goals. Between its founding in 1972 and 2017, in just 45 years the institute has organised more than 575 conferences, training sessions, and educational seminars and meetings of experts, which have been attended by 48,254 jurists from 167 countries and 486 universities. As its role has expanded over the years, it has collaborated with 51 intergovernmental organizations, 55 NGOs, 58 civil society organizations and numerous government bodies. The institute has published more than 149 volumes of scholarly and scientific research, along with conference proceedings.

I was elected secretary-general of the institute in 1972. Since I was already serving as deputy secretary-general of the AIDP, I felt that my career in international criminal law was really taking off.

1997: Bermuda

IN MARCH 1997, my second wife, Nina,[32] and I were in Bermuda, taking a brief break from Chicago's harsh winters, when I received a call from the office of the president of Trinidad and Tobago. President-elect Arthur A.N. Robinson was going to be sworn in on 19 March, the caller said, and he personally insisted that I attend the ceremony.

President-elect Robinson and I had been friends for years; we were working together on the establishment of the international criminal court, and he had been to the Siracusa Institute twice. I accepted, telling the caller that attending would be an honour and a privilege that my wife and I would not want to miss.

Finding a flight to Trinidad was not difficult. The problem was that I had packed only a blue blazer and grey slacks – no suit – and Nina had brought only the summer dresses appropriate for a resort. We knew we would be underdressed, but we also knew that attending the ceremony was what really mattered.

We were greeted at the airport in Trinidad by presidential officials who put us in an official car with a motorcade. I have no idea where they found the two policemen who rode the Harley Davidsons ahead of and behind our car, but the men were huge, at least 6 feet 4. Sirens sounded, traffic parted and we headed for the hotel.

At the hotel we were cautioned that we had only about 20 minutes to change (time, of course, that we did not need), and as we left we pretended not to notice what seemed like surprised looks from the staff – directed, we were sure, at our casual clothes. Our little motorcade then proceeded to the large grounds of the presidential palace.

The dais had a few seats for those who would be with the president as he took the oath of office. Opposite that was a stand for the invited guests, whom I estimated to number at least 1,000, and to the left was another dais labelled 'Heads of State' with about 20 seats. Behind that was a larger stand for diplomats, which already held about 150 people.

---

[32] I married Nina following the end of my first marriage of almost twenty years. Nina and I were married for 23 years.

To our surprise, Nina and I were escorted to the 'Heads of State' dais, where we found our names on two seats in the centre of the second row, behind the presidents of Jamaica and the Bahamas. Because we were among the last to arrive, we (and, I assumed, our dress), attracted some attention.

All the heads of states were wearing dark suits except the president of Jamaica, who contrary to military protocol had added his medals to the civilian suit he was wearing. But he was an imposing figure who looked at me and said, 'Forgive me, but what state are you the head of?'

'I come from Egypt', I said.

He nodded and turned around. Perhaps thirty seconds later he turned around again.

'Are you the president of Egypt?', he asked.

I said, 'I hope to be one day.'

He shook his head, still unsure who I was.

The ceremony was a grand event, as most of these ceremonies are anywhere in the world. When it was over, those from the 'Heads of States' area were the first escorted back to the cars. Back at the hotel, when we realised we would have to appear again, underdressed, at a formal dinner at the president's residence, we were mortified.

The dinner table was fairly long, lined with Caribbean heads of state and their spouses, many of whom wore long dresses. I was still in my blue blazer and grey slacks, and my wife wore her simple summer beach dress. After dinner there were toasts and short speeches, and then President Robinson made a few humorous remarks before personally addressing each head of state.

He then stopped for a few seconds, chuckled a little, and said

I know some of you, if not all, have wondered what this distinguished couple, Professor Cherif Bassiouni and his wife, are doing among Caribbean heads of state. In parliamentary language this is called the point of personal privilege. I consider Cherif the father of international criminal law and one of the makers of the future international criminal court. Cherif is the head of the Siracusa Institute, and there he is considered a head of state.

In the laughter that followed, I felt that I had become part of the group.

July–August 2003: Chicago and Various Cities in Afghanistan

ALWAYS A CURIOUS and precocious child and fortunately a quick learner, I don't remember a time when education has not been a part of my life, from boarding school in Egypt to universities in France, Switzerland, Egypt and then the United States. And once I began teaching, that work, like my schooling, has never been limited to one subject, one institution, one country or even one language.

More than two years before my appointment as Independent Expert on Human Rights in Afghanistan, in late 2001 prominent Afghanis signed the Bonn agreement, creating an interim government after the fall of the Taliban. The agreement called for states to help provide support for the development of specific sectors of Afghani society, and Italy took on the task of justice.

Because of this, in the summer of 2003, as the then-president of the Siracusa Institute, I found myself in Kabul to establish a judge-training course on behalf of the Italian government. Working with the International Development Law Organization (IDLO), we were to conduct training for approximately 400 Afghani judges. The Siracusa Institute would focus on training for criminal matters; the IDLO on civil matters.

Before travelling to Afghanistan, I had developed what I thought would be the most effective approach to this training, which was complicated by many factors far beyond our control, including the fact that 10 per cent of the judges could not read or write and that the majority had only high school diplomas. Our training also had to be effective and useful for people whose tribal laws and customs varied so greatly that the idea of developing a single national training programme for judges from different ethnic backgrounds and different tribal regions often seemed an impossible task. But I had considerable experience conducting judicial training for judges, government officials and others, and I was accompanied by talented and hard-working staff members.

Upon arriving in Kabul, I submitted my academic plan for approval. This plan consisted of dividing the material into small subject matter units and separating the judges into ten groups of 40, who would then all receive the same training, with about two and a half to three days on each subject matter.

To accomplish this training, we would first train a number of non-Afghanis at the Siracusa Institute and then take them all back to Afghanistan, where they would spend about a month in-country to cover the same subject for the ten groups. Training the trainers in Siracusa, we figured, would make recruiting teachers from Egypt, other Arab and Muslim countries, and perhaps even some Western nations much easier.

The day I submitted my written plan to the Afghan Chief Justice Shinwari was the first time he and I met. I went into his spacious office, where some 10–12 Afghanis were already seated. Wearing a long white beard and matching white turban, he got up from his desk to greet me and motioned me to take a seat next to him. I noticed that he was barefoot and that on occasion he would pull his feet to his chair and scratch his toes, which left me rather unsettled and perplexed.

After the initial greetings there was an uncomfortable silence, which I broke by proposing to the chief justice that he review my plan for training the 400 judges in units of ten and mixing the judges from different areas to create some integration and also that he approve the ten subject matters that would be covered during each group's training. He accepted my written report courteously, placed it on his desk, and then, without looking at me, said, 'I only read the Qur'an.'

I replied that it would be very useful if he could designate a member of his staff or another expert to review the programme and give me the benefit of his views. He nodded but did not answer. Then to my surprise, he turned around, looked me in the eye, and said, 'I don't know what you will be teaching these judges, but today I had to personally order two journalists arrested because they criticised some of my actions.'

If the chief justice believed he could send journalists to prison for expressing their views, despite the Afghan constitution's freedom-of-expression provision, taking this action on his own, without any authority under the constitution or the laws of Afghanistan, then I knew I had a long, hard road ahead. But I decided this was a moment to be seized. I looked him straight in the eye and said, 'Mr Chief Justice, you have no legal authority to do so.'

His entire body showed anger, and by the time my statement had been translated for those at the table who did not speak Arabic, murmurs of disapproval floated around the room. The chief justice, with his eyes still fixed furiously on me, said, 'How do you know that?'

I replied that no statement in the new Afghani constitution, nor the laws of the country, gave the chief justice the power of arrest and detention.

He turned to me and said, 'Under *shari'a* law I have that power.'

***

Afghanistan uses the Hanafi school, one of the four schools of Sunni jurisprudence, but the chief justice did not know that I had been a student of *shari'a*, and in particular the Hanafi school, since I had been at law school. During that time, I studied under one of the most celebrated Muslim scholars of the day, Sheikh Muhammad Abu Zahra, who taught me *shari'a* and criminal justice for two years at the University of Cairo. I had continued to be a student of *shari'a*, particularly its criminal aspects.

As I sat in that office, I knew that to deal with the chief justice, I needed first to repress any egotistic manifestation and try to be as humble and modest as I could, so I said only that I had studied the Hanafi school and was one of Sheikh Abu Zahra's students.

He looked at me with profound consternation and then at the others in the room, who all started talking in Pashto at the same time. I could only guess at what was being said. The chief justice then held up his hand to stop the chatter and gave an order to one of the men, who left the room and came back about ten minutes later with eight people of various turban sizes and beard lengths. These men turned out to be judges on the Supreme Court. I did not realise at the time that this was to be my trial.

Fortunately, before leaving Chicago, as I prepared to present my training plan to the chief justice, I had taken some time to look over some of my books on the Hanafi school that I had read many years before. This effort to refresh my memory turned out to be a lifesaver.

Once everyone had been assembled, the chief justice turned to me and asked specifically what I had studied about *shari'a*, which books and articles I had read, which conferences by Abu Zahra I had attended. He then opened up the floor for the eight judges to ask me questions, questions much like those that a police or prosecutor would ask someone under interrogation, even though the subject of the questions were theological. I seemed to acquit myself well on all issues except one, the issue of apostasy, the renunciation of a religious faith, and there we differed quite strongly. For a very long time, I had opposed considering apostasy a crime punishable by death under *shari'a* and particularly under the Hanafi school. Even though my view was contrary to that of many Muslim scholars, enough scholars shared it that it was no longer deemed heretic or discredited but was recognised as a valid, if a minority, view. By the end of my examination, the atmosphere had changed completely. I had become one of them. Sharwani stood up and hugged me and we all went out for lunch as happy comrades.

Before departing, I asked the chief justice if he approved my plan for the training.

'Absolutely, absolutely', he said.

He nodded. Everyone else in the room nodded, too. Then he looked at me and asked, 'Is there anything else you want?'

With temerity that came out nowhere, I responded that we wanted women judges to be allowed in the programme. The chief justice gestured disapprovingly, and once again I was surrounded by the hushed tones of all of those present.

'We have no women judges', the chief justice said. 'Besides, it is contrary to *shari'a*.'

I jokingly said, 'We can save that question for discussion until after lunch, but can you still appoint some women?'

'I will do so', he replied.

Everybody else in the room looked at each other with deep bewilderment.

This was indeed an enormous breakthrough in the history of Afghanistan. Chief Justice Shinwari (who, I learned during lunch, had only a *shari'a* high school diploma) did appoint 50 women, all university graduates, many from foreign universities. But unfortunately – and perhaps predictably – he did not indicate which courts he was appointing them to. So for all practical purposes, they were appointed as judges for the sole purpose of participating in the training programme. I later heard that some were assigned a few judicial functions, but most were not.

With approval in hand and with the appointment of women judges, we began the training programme. In the smaller groups, which included the 50 women, the women markedly influenced the dynamics. Seating was by age: the youngest judges sat together in the first row, while the eldest judges sat in the last rows. (For the most part, the eldest had the least amount of formal education, although this did not necessarily translate to their being the least wise, as there were many very wise tribal judges.) So in each cohort, there was a gender gap, several generational gaps and several education gaps.

In general, the women and the younger judges were the leaders in each of the ten groups and the ones who probably benefited the most from the training. I am not really sure whether these people's experience in the training ever bore fruit in the Afghani system, but I saw it as a positive step for the country.

April 1993: The Former Yugoslavia

IN MID- TO late April 1993, I witnessed a deeply moving sight in Sarajevo, where I was attending a meeting with Zvonimir Šeparović, a professor of criminal law at the University of Zagreb who was the former Croatian minister of foreign affairs.

Our appointment was after sunset, and as my car approached the entrance of the meeting place, I noticed a group of women gathered at a temporarily constructed brick wall. These women, I learned, were called the Mothers of Vukovar. Their sons had allegedly been slaughtered near Vukovar, in Croatia, and they had built a brick wall about four or five feet high. Each brick bore the name of one of the missing sons. On top of the brick wall they had lit candles, and the mothers all stood behind the wall dressed in black. It was a starkly simple, beautiful memorial, and I regret that I didn't have the presence of mind at the time to stop the car and go greet the mothers. I did wonder whether the family of the young Croat professor, the man who had approached me in Siracusa in 1991 and told me about the fighting in his homeland, was among those in the crowd. If his own family wasn't there, surely his neighbours, friends or colleagues were. No one, it seemed, was immune from the conflict's devastating effects.

1969: Chicago and Los Angeles

IN THE YEARS I remained in the United States, my social, personal and professional circles expanded, giving me many friends and colleagues.

But in 1969 I lost my mother, one of the most important people in my life.

When I left Egypt in 1961, I thought that my mother was on the losing side of her battle with cancer, but she soon overcame the disease. But by the mid-1960s, the cancer struck again, and we were told that this time it would be fatal. My mother had kept the little medallion of Saint Thérèse that my Italian nurse had given me back in 1946, when I was ill with diphtheria, and when she became sick she often wore a little gold necklace with a pendant of a small Qur'an and the medallion of Saint Thérèse.

I was asleep in Chicago one night when I woke suddenly. I woke Rossana and told her that something was wrong with my mother.

My mother's husband, Earl Cochran, answered the phone in California and said he had been about to call me. 'I don't think she's going to make it through the night', he said.

I took a red-eye flight and arrived at my mother's house the next morning to find that she had been in a coma for about two hours. Her room was dark, and her German shepherd was sitting by her bedside. As soon as I entered the room, my mother opened one dark eye; she had not been able to see out of the other one for some time.

'I'm glad that you came', she said. 'It took all that I had to keep on going to wait for you, and I just wanted to see you one more time.' I hugged my mother, and she died in my arms.

At my mother's request, we held a very intimate ceremony in a non-denominational chapel before burying her in Westwood Village Memorial Park Cemetery. The only people attending were her husband, Earl, Rossana and me, and Professor Haroun Haddad and his wife, Leila. The Haddads – and how they re-entered my life – are reminders of how I try to live each day: help others, use your gifts and circumstances to better the lives of those in need, and remember that fate – God's will, whatever you want to call it – will ensure that the right circumstances present themselves. And for me, as they did in this case, things usually come full circle.

* * *

In the later part of his life, my father became a naturalized US citizen and moved to Chicago in 1971, though he continued to spend time in Egypt. He died on 24 May 1995, in Alexandria, Egypt.

2009: Paris

My life has been full of circles.

Saint Thérèse of Lisieux, whose medallion was pinned to my pyjamas when I was saved from diphtheria at age eight, and I connected for a second time more than sixty years later.

My third wife, Elaine,[33] and I were together in Paris that year. Tired from our travels (I had come from Siracusa, Italy, Elaine from Chicago), we decided to take an afternoon nap in the suite that a kind hotel manager had upgraded us to because our regular room had not been ready.

Suddenly, as clearly as if I had been awake, I saw Saint Thérèse standing in front of me, holding the bouquet of flowers that I had seen her carrying in the shrine in Cairo. I cannot remember exactly what she said to me in the dream, but the gist was, 'Isn't it about time you visited me?'

I awoke to find that although the curtains were still drawn, light had somehow flooded the room. Frightened at first, I looked at the spot where she had been standing and walked around the room – and of course found nothing. After I finished my inspection, the light left and the room was dark again.

'Holy moly', was all I could think.

As soon as Elaine woke, I told her we were going to Lisieux the next day, saying I would explain later.

The next morning, after the short train ride to Lisieux, when we climbed the stairs to enter the cathedral, we were essentially alone. I approached Saint Thérèse's statue, similar to the one I had seen in Cairo showing her holding a bouquet of flowers, smiled at her, and said, 'Well, I'm here.'

As if she had been sent to deliver the news, a nun appeared and told me that Saint Thérèse was actually buried on the site and I could visit her sarcophagus downstairs. I walked down to the sarcophagus, said a little prayer, apologised for being late, thanked her for what she had done for me, prayed that she would stick by me, and then said my goodbye. As we walked out of the cathedral, tourists from about ten buses streamed into the church.

---

[33] Elaine and I were married a few years after the death of my second wife, Nina. She remains by my side to this day.

Elaine and I stopped to eat at a restaurant, but I was so stunned by what had happened that for some time I couldn't speak. 'Is it my imagination', I finally managed to say, 'Or was the church empty for me and then when I finished my visit, it became full?' Elaine said that certainly had been her impression, too.

From the moment I saw Saint Thérèse in the Paris hotel room, I felt her presence. I felt her when I stepped in the church, and when I went down to where she was buried. I think I must have felt her throughout my entire life, but not as vividly as in those moments. I can still feel the difference, as great as that between night and day, from the moment that I went to bed with the little medallion, when my mother, aunt and nurse sat in my room, looking as if they were watching over a dead person, and the next morning. That night I was half-gone, in the twilight world of half-death and half-here. Then the next day, there was no trace of the diphtheria, and I felt as good as ever.

Ever since that day, I felt as if I had been saved, but only for the moment. From then on, I always felt that I would die of some kind of heart failure, and in my last few years I have struggled with a heart condition. This has given me the sense that life operates in circles, and there is a certain harmony about it. My being placed under house arrest, for example, heightened my fear of torture, and then God gave me the opportunity to help draft the UN Convention against Torture.

1963: Los Angeles

ROSSANA AND I honeymooned in Hawaii. On our way west, we stopped in California to see my mother, who by then was married to a dentist named Earl Cochran and had purchased a lovely house on Sunset Boulevard from Eva Gabor, the sister of Zsa Zsa. On our first day there, I borrowed my mother's car to go to Malibu beach, which I had seen in the movies. It is an easy drive – just keep going on Sunset Boulevard until you get there. I walked with my new wife along the famous boardwalk that has been featured in so many Hollywood movies and is always full of tourists.

It was sunset. People were all over the boardwalk and on the beach below. I rushed ahead to the end of the boardwalk to be near the water and to admire the changing colours of the sky. Sitting on a bench nearby was an older gentleman who seemed rather tall but was hunched over. I thought he looked familiar. I walked over to him, and sure enough, saw that he was Professor Haroun Haddad, the same Professor Haddad who had taught me at the Jesuit boarding school and whom I had tried to help avoid deportation from Egypt all those many years ago. He was as stunned then as he had been when I had bumped into him in Cairo in 1956. Once again, he had tears in his eyes, and so did I. We hugged each other for a long time.

I introduced him to Rossana, merely saying that he had been my teacher in three high school history courses when I was at the Jesuit College of the Holy Family. After the usual social niceties, Professor Haddad turned toward me and asked, 'Do you remember my youngest son?', and I told him of course I remembered him. The son, he said, was coming to pick him up and drive him home. Could Rossana and I follow his son so that his wife, Leila, could see me and meet my wife? To my surprise, I learned that the Haddads lived in Westwood, just a few blocks from the University of California's campus, where Professor Haddad taught, and just a few minutes from my mother's house. The coincidences were almost unbelievable.

When we arrived at the Haddads' apartment and Leila (or, as I called her, Mrs Haddad) saw me, she had tears in her eyes. She hugged me affectionately, sat us down and proceeded to tell Rossana that I was a true friend who had stood up for them in their time of need, even though it meant facing the wrath of Egypt's dictatorial regime.

Somewhat embarrassed and not really thinking about what I was saying, I blurted out, 'What was their reason?', which I realised later could have been misinterpreted but fortunately was not.

Professor Haddad replied, 'Once again, you touch me deeply, because you saw me as an Egyptian, a teacher and someone you looked up to, and you had no thoughts about anything else.' He was my teacher, whom I happened to like and respect and who knew and admired my grandfather – what else should matter? Whether he was Jewish, Muslim, Christian or atheist made no difference to me. Somehow in the chance meeting, I felt a new connection to him and Leila. Our relationship deepened, despite how little time we had together.

We had tea and talked about many things concerning Egypt. Professor Haddad told me he had left Cairo for a Jewish resettlement camp in Genoa to await his transfer to Paris, where he had sought to be permanently resettled. Between the Jewish organisation that took care of him and his family and the Jesuits in France, he was able to reach Paris in three months, get a job teaching in a French high school, and pursue a PhD at the Sorbonne. A few years later, with this doctoral degree, he taught at a small French university and then was able to find a job at the University of California, Los Angeles, where he taught history in the Middle East Department. His oldest son, who had been my classmate all through high school, went to medical school in the United States and then opened a private practice in West Los Angeles.

After Rossana and I left the Haddads' apartment, we returned to my mother's house and told her the story. My mother immediately invited the Haddads for dinner. Although they were strangers, Leila Haddad and my mother instantly liked each other, and they became very close in the years to come. Our families shared a unique, unwavering bond.

2015: Chicago

THROUGHOUT MY LIFE, perhaps because of my sense of spirituality, I have had a sense of destiny. Even as a young man, I always felt that I was destined to do something important. Now, reaching my 78th birthday as I write this, I would not dare say that I'm disappointed, as I would not want to seem ungrateful to God, but what I feel is certainly not the sense of accomplishment that I envisioned.

I find it difficult to be in the decline of my life and no longer centre stage. I imagine that this happens to a lot of people, perhaps more in America than in Europe and the Arab world, where younger people still honour and revere the elderly. But every once in a while, I have these sorts of feelings, and I have to learn how to live with them and to accept and prepare for the inevitability of the end of my journey here on earth.

It's not an easy thing to face, but as I come to this point, I realise that I have spent so much of my life running forward, as in the days of my youth, fervently forward, rushing to fulfil the sense of destiny that drove me. I never really had much time to stop to think about things, to reflect on the end of one stage or the start of another. So it is now, in my old age, that I look back, cautiously, even timidly, at times because I don't know what I'm going to see, and then try to evaluate and assess my life's experiences.

As human beings, we all need to feel gratification for the work we do in life. We need to feel success, whether it's in large or small things. Sometimes I say to myself, 'Okay. You went to that ceremony, and they gave you an honorary degree or medal, and you were happy for about two days. And then what?'

I am still active in my field, and so to that extent I still have one foot in the limelight. But there is going to come a time where I will take myself entirely out of that world, and the line separating the part of my life that was active and productive from the part of my life that is evaluative and introspective will come. It's not easy to think about the final stage of life, but I do believe that this stage must be a reflective period, a period where I find serenity.

I believe that the best way to leave this world is to leave it serenely, without bitterness or desire for things that you have not yet accomplished, and with no ill feelings toward any person or any part of your life's experiences. This is what it means to be at peace with yourself and with the universe.

Index